assigned: life with gender

the society pages

the
society
pages

assigned: life with gender

lisa wade, guest editor

OCCIDENTAL COLLEGE

douglas hartmann

UNIVERSITY OF MINNESOTA

christopher uggen

UNIVERSITY OF MINNESOTA

w. w. norton & company

NEW YORK | LONDON

W. W. Norton & Company has been independent since its founding in 1923, when William Warder Norton and Mary D. Herter Norton first published lectures delivered at the People's Institute, the adult education division of New York City's Cooper Union. The firm soon expanded its program beyond the Institute, publishing books by celebrated academics from America and abroad. By mid-century, the two major pillars of Norton's publishing program—trade books and college texts—were firmly established. In the 1950s, the Norton family transferred control of the company to its employees, and today—with a staff of four hundred and a comparable number of trade, college, and professional titles published each year—W. W. Norton & Company stands as the largest and oldest publishing house owned wholly by its employees.

Book Design: Isaac Tobin
Composition: Westchester Book Composition
Manufacturing: RR Donnelley - Harrisonburg
Production Manager: Sean Mintus

ISBN: 978-0-393-28445-4

Library of Congress Cataloging-in-Publication Data

Title: Assigned : life with gender / Lisa Wade, Guest Editor, Occidental
    College, Douglas Hartmann, University of Minnesota, Christopher Uggen,
    University of Minnesota.
Description: New York : W. W. Norton & Company, Inc., 2016. | Series: The
    society pages | Includes bibliographical references and index.
Identifiers: LCCN 2016000658 | ISBN 9780393284454 (pbk.)
Subjects: LCSH: Sex role. | Feminism. | Sex discrimination against women. |
    Gender identity.
Classification: LCC HQ1075 .A88 2016 | DDC 305.3—dc23 LC record
available at http://lccn.loc.gov/2016000658

W. W. Norton & Company, Inc., 500 5th Avenue, New York, NY 10110-0017

www.wwnorton.com

W. W. Norton & Company, Ltd., Castle House, 75/76 Wells Street, London
W1T3QT

thesocietypages.org

contents

part 5 the future of gender

series preface

DOUGLAS HARTMANN AND CHRISTOPHER UGGEN

t started with a conversation about record labels. Our favorite imprints are known for impeccable taste, creative design, and an eye for both quality and originality. Wouldn't it be cool if W. W. Norton & Company and TheSocietyPages.org joined forces to develop a book series with the same goals in mind? Namely, to consistently deliver the best work by the most original voices in the field.

The Society Pages (TSP) is a multidisciplinary online hub bringing fresh social scientific knowledge and insight to the broadest public audiences in the most open, accessible, and timely manner possible. The largest, most visible collection of sociological material on the web (currently drawing about one million readers per month), TSP is composed of a family of prolific blogs and bloggers, podcasts, interviews, exchanges, teaching content, reading recommendations, and original features like There's Research on That! (TROT!), Clippings, Discoveries, and Office Hours podcasts. The TSP book series, published in collaboration with W. W. Norton, assembles the best original content from in and around the website in key thematic collections. With contributions from leading scholars and a provocative collection of discussion topics and group activities, this innovative series provides an accessible and affordable entry point for strong sociological perspectives on topics of immediate social import and public relevance.

Volume 6 of TSP's book series addresses gender, broadly and ecumenically defined. In a change from our first five TSP books, we recruited prolific public scholar Lisa Wade—founder and principal author of the blockbuster blog *Sociological Images* (housed on The Society Pages), co-author of *Gender: Ideas, Interactions, Institutions* (W. W. Norton, 2014), and sociologist at Occidental College—as a guest editor. Wade went on to select 34 essays from The Society Pages and all around the web for the volume. Among the authors and pieces included, you will find activists, scholars, and journalists, some well-known, others up-and-coming, and each with a distinctive perspective and powerful voice. Together, they present a revealing picture of gender in the United States today: socially constructed, sometimes fun but almost always problematic, fluid but forced into binaries, deeply held but often misunderstood.

The selections are slotted into five sections: Ideas, Performances, Inequalities, Institutions, and The Future. Building upon Wade's popular gender textbook from W. W. Norton, this organizational scheme provides a theoretical logic that both captures the depth and complexity of gender as a social system and is eminently sociological.

The first set of chapters in the book is all about ideas. Using topics ranging from parenting and sexuality to sports and breasts (both men's and women's), they show, at a most basic level, how gender is constructed and how deeply it shapes so many aspects of our lives. More than this, the chapters explore the cultural assumptions and stereotypes about women and men's roles in society, and the masculine and feminine characteristics we so frequently associate with them.

The next section is on performances. It begins from the proposition that ideas about gender don't just exist but must be constantly produced, reproduced, and reinforced in actual social life and human interaction. The activities detailed here range from everyday things like talk and dress to the forces that compel women and men to behave in different and distinct ways in families, on the big screen, and at work. But the overarching point is that gender exists in behavior as much as belief; it is something that must be "done."

Why do ideas about and performances of gender matter so much? Because they help us understand how inequalities and injustices in contemporary social life are so stubbornly and systematically reproduced. This is the focus of the pieces collected in the section on inequalities, the terrain that sociologists of gender are best-known for among scholars and the public. In these chapters—which take on topics ranging from biased science and teaching evaluations to bad bar behavior, feminism, and Miley Cyrus—we see that gender is not just about being different or even being treated differently, but also about systematic unfairness, inequality, and stratification. This theme is extended with the chapters on institutions in the fourth section of the book. Here we see how gender inequalities are reproduced in large-scale, organized dimensions of social life such as health care, the military, education, media, and fashion.

The final set of chapters looks to the future of gender. Not only do these chapters anticipate what the future may hold for gendered identities, images, situations, and inequalities, they help us to imagine a better future—and the role each one of us might play in helping to bring such changes in the gender order. This is sociology at its finest, where analysis meets action and critical thinking is translated into recipes for actual social change.

The volume concludes with a TSP Discussion Guide and Group Activities section that challenges readers to draw connections among the chapters, think more deeply and critically about gender and social life, and link to ongoing conversations and interactive posts online.

Before we turn things over to Professor Wade for her introductory remarks, we want to express our gratitude, as always, to the University of Minnesota, W. W. Norton & Company (in particular, the sociology editor, Sasha Levitt, and her visionary predecessor, Karl Bakeman), and The Society Pages' graduate student board. Evan Stewart and Jacqui Frost are our project's graduate editors. Suzy McElrath created the graphics used throughout this volume, and Anne Kaduk and Frost assisted Wade directly in the work of choosing and organizing the pieces in this volume and producing the discussion materials in the conclusion. Our associate editor and producer is the incomparable Letta Page, whose talents are evident on each page of these volumes and TheSocietyPages.org.

introduction: sex shocker! men and women aren't that different

LISA WADE

Somewhere in the deep, dark depths of the ocean, a male anglerfish is hungry. He lacks the artificial, bioluminescent lure that females use to attract prey. This is a rather insignificant problem compared to the fact that he is incapable of digesting food.

The only bite he'll ever take will be a love bite. He'll latch on to a female anglerfish with his teeth, triggering a chemical reaction that will dissolve his face and fuse him permanently to his female counterpart. Eventually he'll lose every organ in his body to this process—except his testicles. Those will stick around, literally. A happy female anglerfish is dotted with pairs of balls, safe deposit boxes of sperm that she draws on at will.

This is sexual dimorphism. The phrase refers to the degree to which males and females of a species differ. Anglerfish are obviously strongly dimorphic. Males and females of some species, like the ring-necked dove, are almost impossible to tell apart. In the big scheme of things, humans are more like ring-necked doves than anglerfish, though we seem hell-bent on ignoring that.

Instead, we obsess over gender differences. We search for them in scientific studies, scour religious texts for hints from a higher power, and extrapolate from the behavior of our friends and loved ones. We write and read a seemingly endless stream of books counting and discounting the evidence. We argue over whether the differences we think we see are caused by nature or nurture.

When it all comes down to it, though, how much difference are we talking about?

If we were as sexually dimorphic as the elephant seal, the average human male would tower six feet above the average woman and weigh 550 pounds. If we were like gorillas, men and women would be about the same height as they are now, but the average man would outweigh the average woman by over 166 pounds.

If we were as sexually dimorphic as the blanket octopus, men would be 0.8% the size of a female (about the size of a walnut). If we were green spoonworms, the average human male would be less than an inch tall and he would live his entire life inside a female's digestive tract.

If we were as sexually dimorphic as the Alaskan moose, men would walk around with antlers four feet six inches wide, but only during mating season. If human males were like the rhinoceros beetle, they would sport a single horn that protruded almost four feet. That might be inconvenient.

It would be lovely, though, if men carried lustrous manes like male lions or were covered in iridescent, glossy, shimmery skin that changed colors as they turned in the light, as many birds do. It might be quite pretty if they preened 11-foot tails that tripled their body length, like the resplendent quetzal; even better if they could advertise their romantic interest with a display like the peacock. I wouldn't mind.

Nor would I complain about being drab if the boys came in dramatic colors. If we were as sexually dimorphic as Northern cardinals, men would be bright red with a black mask around their eyes and throat and women would look pretty much as they do now. But we don't have to let the boys be the pretty ones. We could be like eclectus parrots: boys in bright green and blue, girls in purple and red.

Some sorts of sexual dimorphism are less appealing. If we were as sexually dimorphic as orangutans, males would be distinguished from females by large, fatty cheek flaps from temple to chin. If we were like the proboscis monkey, a guy would have a rather massive bulbous nose that started between his eyes and hung several inches below his mouth. If we took after the platypus, men would be poisonous, with a spur on their foot that could inject venom. Luckily for the ladies, they would probably only use it on each other; it appears to be mostly a way to compete for females.

As Dorothy Sayers once said: "[W]omen are more like men than anything else in the world." Yes, we're different. We reproduce sexually, so we do come in two (with some exceptions) types: one that potentially gestates, births, and feeds new life, and one that can mix up the genes of our species. Most men don't have a uterus, and most women will never inseminate anyone.

But we're not *that* different. It's kind of amazing when you think about it. We face a great deal of pressure to be different. We live in a world in which "men are from Mars and women are from Venus" is a household phrase, but scholars find little to no difference on 78% of traits, abilities, interests, attitudes, and behaviors. As communications scholar Kathryn Dindia once put it, it'd be more correct to say, "Men are from North Dakota, women are from South Dakota." We are alike despite ourselves.

"Opposite sexes," then, is obviously a misnomer. The phrase suggests that men and women are fundamentally dissimilar. In fact, if we have to choose between arguing that we are exactly the same and totally different, we have to go with the former. We are much more alike than we are different. Still, gender is meaningful to us and affects our lives as *if* the differences are more substantial than they really are. In this book, we'll get a sense of how.

A version of this article originally appeared on Salon *on September 18, 2013.*

exhibit one

"Just because you live in fear for your life doesn't mean you let yourself go, ladies!" That was the snarky introduction to writer Ariane Lange's Buzzfeed collection of fictional female TV and movie characters who, despite an absence of any semblance of modern conveniences, still manage to shave their armpits. Her first examples were Ginger and Mary Ann in the 1960s classic *Gilligan's Island*. When a real woman "gets lost at sea," Lange wrote, "her razor gets lost with her."

She also features examples from *Planet of the Apes, The Blue Lagoon, Beauty and the Beast, Alien, Waterworld, Lost,* and *The Hunger Games.* How *do* women supposedly shave on deserted islands? Did the Beast slip Belle a razor? Did Ripley in *Alien,* one of the most badass women in cinema, really feel insecure about the appearance of her armpits?

We see it even on *The Walking Dead,* a show that is almost intolerably realistic. The producers go to great lengths to portray what a zombie apocalypse might be like. They are especially keen on the nasty bits: what it looks like when dead people don't die, what it looks like to kill the undead, the evil this all spawns in those left alive. It's gruesome. The show is a gore orgy. But armpit hair on women? Apparently that would be *too* gross.

All those shiny armpits are a great example of how reality—the fact that both men and women tend to have hair under their armpits—sometimes loses out to ideology, or what we *want* to believe is true about men and women.

exhibit two

"There've been a lot of men that I've worked with that I don't wear shoes with," actress Kelly McGillis told a reporter. Her remark came in response to a question about working with Tom Cruise in *Top Gun*. McGillis is five foot ten, and Cruise, at five foot seven, is short for a guy. You'd never notice if you watched his movies, though. He seems to stand an inch or two taller than his female costars in *Mission: Impossible III* (Michelle Monaghan, also five foot seven), *Knight and Day* (Cameron Diaz, five foot nine), *Oblivion* (Olga Kurylenko, five foot eight), and so on. Like other leading men who come up short, Cruise wears high heels—ahem, "lifts"—or stands on boxes. Their leading women slump, sit, and stay in their stockings.

Men are a few inches taller than women on average, but some women are taller than some men. In the movies, though, the fiction that women never tower over men is carefully cultivated. They try to cast romantic coleads who affirm our belief in tall men and short women. And when they can't, they film scenes so that the audience will never know their hero's little secret.

exhibit three

In Greco-Roman wrestling, boxing, and mixed martial arts, there is a rule that you never hit "below the belt." The area of biggest concern is the testicles. Even the Ultimate Fighting Championship specifies that "groin attacks of any kind" are a foul. This is probably because groin attacks might make for short fights, and, in any case, the skills being tested are of a different kind.

These rules, though, have the notable, if unintended, effect of *protecting* our belief in male strength. What would fights look like if one *could* go below the belt? There'd be a lot more collapsing and writhing in pain and a lot less getting up. All in all, it would add up to less time looking powerful and more time looking pitiful, sending a clear message that men's bodies are *vulnerable*.

Not hitting below the belt, then, protects the idea that men's bodies are fighting machines and that men are big, strong, and impenetrable. The rule against punching and kicking testicles doesn't just protect men, it protects our *ideas about* men.

———

All these examples—about hair, height, and hitting below the belt—illustrate that the ideas about men and women that we encounter don't necessarily match reality. We call these ideas *stereotypes*, preconceived notions about particular kinds of people. Gender stereotypes are the collections of characteristics that we attribute to people depending on the configuration of their genitals. We generally call those collections *masculinity* and *femininity*.

We attribute masculinity and femininity to people with male and female bodies, respectively. Men are strong, tall, and hairy. Women are small, smooth, and vulnerable. We call each other *opposite* sexes, discursively insisting that whatever men are, women aren't and whatever women are, men aren't.

Oddly, we also attribute masculinity and femininity to many of the things around us: cats and dogs, wine and beer, ballet and breakdancing. We say meat is for men and vegetables for women, even though we all know that a balanced meal contains both protein and vitamins. We make the whole world obey a *gender binary*, a separation of everything into two different and contrasting gendered boxes.

The essays in this section are about those boxes. Why do we feel compelled by them? How do we adapt and resist? Who struggles? And why? But first, how do we learn the size and shape of the boundaries our culture puts around gender?

—LISA WADE

on queering parenting and gender-neutrality

D'LANE COMPTON AND TRISTAN BRIDGES

B ecoming a parent is fascinating, but becoming a parent who studies gender and sexuality and—for one of us—identifies as queer . . . well, let's just say that creates a whole different level of awareness and curiosity. Prior to becoming parents, we both had a fine-tuned appreciation of the ways that gender and sexuality structure experiences and opportunities.

Anne Fausto-Sterling draws a great metaphor comparing the onset of gender binaries to the process of water erosion. At first, the erosion (read: gender) may not be visible. Small, watery tributaries begin to form—the arms of future rivers that could, at this stage, easily change route. Gradually, streams emerge, slowly becoming rivers. And before long, you end up with something like the Grand Canyon. Yet, looking at the Grand Canyon disguises all of the crises that the fledgling streams navigated—watery paths whose flow, course, and geography were yet to be determined. Gender, said Fausto-Sterling, is no different. It takes time to learn to think of it as permanent and predetermined. . . .

Just to put this in context, let us provide an example illustrating this issue as well as the sociological imagination of children at work. It involves a trip to the grocery store, a bold three-year-old girl and her mother. At the checkout line, the girl trotted up to Tristan's cart with her mother, pointed at Tristan's son, and asked her mother, "Is that little baby a boy or a baby girl?" The mother looked to Tristan. He smiled, revealing nothing. "That's . . . um . . . a boy, honey," the mother responded, with a questioning tone (guarding, we assume, for the possibility of having mistaken a *him* for a *her*). "Why?" the little girl asked. Rolling her eyes at Tristan, the mother looked down and gave that classic parenting response— "Because!" she said. "Will he always be a boy?" she continued. The mother chuckled, shrugging her shoulders. "Yes, honey," she laughed, "He'll always be a boy." And with that, they moved on.

. . . Some of the most important lessons we teach children are probably not on purpose—showing them what's worthy of attention, what to ignore, what should be noticed but not discussed, and more. This little girl learned one of the ways that we think about gender in this culture—as a permanent state of being. To think otherwise, she learned, is laughable, though this little girl seemed to understand gender as a young stream capable of becoming many different rivers. Her mother seemed equally sure that the stream had a predetermined path. And here's where things get tricky—they're both right. It's likely Tristan's son will identify as a boy (and, later on, as a man). Most boys do. But treating this process as inevitable disguises the fact that . . . well . . . it's not. This question came out of a three-year-old because she's in the process of acquiring what psychologists refer to as "gender constancy"—an understanding of gender as [fixed]. These beliefs are institutionalized throughout our culture in ways that don't make interactions like these completely predetermined, but make them much more likely.

With the news of a new child, D'Lane feels certain she's somewhere in the stream, while Tristan is beginning to see the emergence of branches that are starting to feel more likely than others. Yet, both of us feel the slow creep of the Grand Canyon. We have lectured for nearly 10 years on how gendering begins prior to birth. "Do you know the sex yet?" is one of the top two questions asked by most people. As a part of a same-sex couple, D'Lane experiences these questions as even more telling.

Prior to birth, we organize names, nurseries, and language to prepare. One of the biggest reasons folks offer to justify their inquiries about the sex of babies before they're born (when they do so) is largely gift-related. And the market for parenting and baby supplies structurally invites the question in more than a few ways and is a powerful force in reproducing our cultural understandings of gender.

"gender-neutrality" and baby gear

A great deal of marketing research must have gone into figuring out exactly what parents mean when they say they want "gender-neutral" clothes, toys, diaper bags, and all variety of baby and parenting paraphernalia. We'd guess that the meanings are pretty straightforward, and we'd imagine if you pressed parents, most would offer a sort of "Not too girlie for a boy" response rather than vice versa (which—if true— would be interesting in and of itself). Through this process, colors like yellow and green have become the default "gender-neutral" colors, so if someone has elected to not find out what their child's genitals look like in the womb, there's a line of products people can feel comfortable purchasing without worrying that they might have bought something "gender transgressive."

And it's not just colors; just about anything can acquire gendered meaning. . . . "Boy" clothes and objects display animals like dogs, lions, bears, dragons, any of the big cats or pachyderms. Meanwhile, "girl" clothes and objects are littered with kittens, unicorns, horses, butterflies, and dolphins.

"Gender-neutral" lines that want to use animals end up selecting from an odd assortment of what's left over—foxes, hedgehogs, owls, turtles, armadillos, and a strange selection of animals that don't have enough of a cultural reputation for violence that might make them "boyish," but are simultaneously not "girlie" enough either. But, the prototypical gender-neutral animal is the duck. In fact, if you ask for gender-neutral items before a baby shower, prepare yourself for ducks.

Patterns also become gendered. Through personal experience with gendered gifting, it follows that stripes are masculine, as is camouflage (unless it's pink). Stars and hearts are feminine, as are rainbows. Results from a quick Google search show that geometric shapes and lines are considered masculine, while polka dots, floral patterns, and scripts are feminine. There's also a trend in bold colors vs. pastels for boys and girls, respectively.

Gender-neutral clothes are easily available for the tiniest babies—presumably for those parents who elect not to "find out." Though there's not a huge selection, and almost all of it is yellow and depicts ducks, most stores in which you can buy for babies six months and younger have a selection of items whose gender is not immediately apparent. As babies get bigger, however, gender-neutral options shrink—or perhaps more accurately, they migrate. Toddler-dom, for instance, is a life stage at which it's increasingly difficult to find much that doesn't scream "boy" or "girl." It's a niche that some of the more upscale stores and labels have been keen to occupy. This is one part of a slow process during which those fledgling streams begin to ossify into more predictable paths.

gendering parenting paraphernalia

As parents, we're also being re-socialized into new roles (mothers, fathers, and more) that subtly invite/compel us to take up certain gendered behaviors, roles, and gender-marked objects and clothing as well. Parenting gear is increasingly as gendered as the objects we buy for our children.

Parenting gear has only recently emerged as a more sex-segregated market. New parenting "stuff" allows parents to consider how a diaper bag reflects their own gender identity and whether couples might require separate gear. There also seems to have been a sudden increase in the diversity of parenting gear available at all. This could be a byproduct of what feels like an increasing diversification of parenting philosophies. There have always been different ideas about what's "right" for babies and what the "right" and "wrong" ways are to raise a child—but it feels like these ideas are becoming more polarized and/or parents of different philosophies are subtly encouraged to be at war with one another. And it's significant that this is often referred to as the "Mommy Wars," a label that casually implies men are largely able to avoid the "fight," [perhaps] because, while we assume that women will have one of an increasing diversity of parenting philosophies, we presume that men parent in one way (if we're lucky enough to have them parenting much at all).

As men have begun playing larger roles in the parenting process—or, at the very least, are culturally expected to—parenting gear for men has emerged as well. Diaper bags, burp clothes, sippy cups, and more are now made with the consideration that men might have to lug them around too. Our brief survey of "daddy-specific gear" found that it really comes in two varieties (which often overlap): it's either less practical than the "feminine" gear (which is, somewhat ironically, exactly the opposite of how it is marketed), or it's simply offensive.

For instance, companies like Diaper Dude market bags specifically to men. The website for Diaper Dude [reads]:

Diaper Dude, created by Chris Pegula, is a movement that began after the birth of the first of his three children by turning feminine-style diaper bags into ones that dads would want to carry. Pegula noticed that most diaper bags and accessories sold at retail stores were designed with women's sense of style in mind. Instead of carrying his baby stuff around in a gym bag or backpack, Pegula created The Diaper Dude for dads.

While the Diaper Dude appears to be a fairly reasonable option for parents who want colorful options without the "feminine" patterns, it is also a smaller bag. It will be great for afternoon excursions or quick outings to the store, but appears to not be designed as an "everyday" diaper and child care bag. Its size highlights a number of cultural assumptions, one of which is that *dudes* won't be primary caretakers—at least in larger increments of time that might necessitate bigger bags.

Using the diaper bag as a sort of case study, some of our examples include what we call the "Construction Bag" and the "Combat Daddy Bag." There's more than one bag that fits each of these patterns, and most are too expensive to only qualify as "gag gifts."

Consider the Combat Daddy Equipment Bag, a product that implicitly draws a connection between child care and war. Indeed, it's a cultural trope that's amassed a small industry. Vin Diesel's portrayal of a Navy SEAL forced into his most difficult mission yet (becoming a parent) in Disney's *The Pacifier* played on this same cultural narrative. That Vin

Diesel initially finds himself woefully unsuited to the task might superficially appear to honor the hard work that women do: *even* a Navy SEAL would struggle with the multitasking and time management required of good parenting. Yet, the story was not of Vin Diesel becoming a "mom," but of finding ways of masculinizing parenting [to] deploy his SEAL skills in a new setting. . . .

The idea that one may not know what they will be dealing with or what "equipment" might be needed, that a man couldn't solve an issue without a shed of tools and material on their backs, as if going camping or into battle when dealing with children, is offensive. Neither does this critique consider the offensiveness toward all the women taking care of children while their men are unavailable due to actual military deployment.

Parenting products like these emerge out of a climate that asks women to "let him do it (t)his way" while subtly telling both men and women that "he" will inevitably parent differently from (and with less competence than) "her." In fact, prior to the emergence of parenting books for men, there was often a section for men in parenting books for women—or a section "about men" for women to read. . . .

"Men's" parenting products help reproduce a cultural narrative that conceals the actual *work* that goes into care work by presenting women as naturally having "it." Others have to compensate for intrinsic deficiencies with all variety of gadgetry.

toward a queer revolution of parenting

But what about parents who might not want the typical patterns of the classic "mom" look, but also might not want to be less functional or use the more kitschy daddy gear? Are there gender-neutral parenting paraphernalia options available? Can Diaper Dude fulfill their desires too?

Gender-neutral baby clothes and toys, just like the recent push toward "daddy" gear, relies on a partial understanding of how gender works. Objects acquire a gender, but are also gendered in how we use, display, play with, and contest them. So, calling a onesie "gender-neutral" or referring to a diaper bag as a "daddy diaper bag" presents gender as though it resides within the objects. This takes our attention away from the fact that we reproduce these meanings in how we use and display these objects, which conceals our ability to challenge the meanings in how they are used as well.

There is a lot to say about how parenting objects and paraphernalia are used in ways that might challenge their meanings. The construction diaper bag is a great example. Comments on Amazon indicate that items like this might often be a gift that women are buying for men. Yet, what would this bag mean if worn by a gay dad (inviting a comparison with the play on masculinity that made the Village People famous)? What would it mean if worn by a woman? Is the product suddenly "queered" in how it's been used?

But even things that are moving away from pink and blue can acquire different meanings when "queered" by the parents making use of them. For instance, Timbuk2 sells a diaper messenger bag (the Stork) marketed with images of men and women whose gender displays are marginally transgressive. In fact, when D'Lane first saw it she was stoked that most of the pictures online showed a diversity of gender. She believed it might be something queer and [Timbuk2] could even potentially be marketing to queer parents. Like gender-neutral clothing for children, [though], the Stork is being marketed to a specific group: the ad depicts only white parents and children, and the cost implies that it's being sold to middle- and upper-middle-class parents. The video detailing the bag's specifics, however—like most of the bags marketed to men—focuses more on practicality, including a joke about carrying around a beer for dad (referred to as "daddy's milk" in the ad) in one of the many compartments. Here, the androgynous non-gendered bag, through language alone, becomes masculinized.

The images and the video are participating in marketing this product in two ways. In some ways, the Stork is being marketed no differently than the Diaper Dude, Combat Daddy, or Construction Daddy—it's being sold to men who might want a diaper bag that doesn't make them feel emasculated. But men aren't the only ones who might desire a less feminine bag. Images of parents with more transgressive gender displays market this product more covertly to parents who might desire to create new models of care, working to illustrate that a capacity to engage in care work can come in a variety of different "packages"—or gender performances, if you prefer. This subtle dual marketing of the Stork Messenger is an illustration of our capacity to play with the meanings and gender of objects.

Thus, new products "for men" might be read as offensive. But the agency of consumers allows for a queer revolution in parenting roles and identities in which these objects provide the raw materials. Queering parenting is a cultural process that actively considers the ways in which parenting practices and identities can resist heteronormative assumptions that structure predominant parenting forms and relations. There is an exciting potential embodied within these practices to become an agent of change.

Considering how this all relates to Anne Fausto-Sterling's comparison is instructive when thinking about long-term change. There are many ways in which we—and others—can intervene in the process of the formation of landscapes. For instance, there are many things we can do to encourage young streams to flow in certain directions and avoid others, but we're also capable of challenging, re-routing, and even halting massive rivers. And we're not alone. If we're metaphorically considering rivers as gender, we can also metaphorically consider consumers as beavers. Beavers are capable of dramatically altering the flow, look, use, and geography of rivers and lakes. It's what they do best. But it is also a slow and tenuous process. It takes time and incredible collaboration. Consider the largest known beaver dam, located in Canada's Wood Buffalo National Park. . . . To quote one *Discovery News* article, beavers are "re-engineering the landscape." We should be taking notes!

This article originally appeared on YourQueerProf.com *on March 21, 2013.*

tits (the story of my man-boobs)

MATT CORNELL

Of the many nicknames I've acquired over the years, there's one I'm reminded of today. The name was given to me by a bully shortly after I entered the sixth grade. I had been a fat kid since elementary school, but as puberty began to kick in, parts of me started growing differently than expected. The doctors said I had gynecomastia—"man boobs," or "moobs" in the jeering parlance of our popular culture.

But my bully simply called them "tits." And so this became my name in the school hallways.

I was Tits.

He would pass me in the hall and catcall "Hey, Tits!" and his buddies would laugh. Sometimes, if he was feeling extra bold, he might actually grab one of my breasts and squeeze it in front of the other kids. Not everyone laughed. But many did.

As direct as this bullying was, growing up with gynecomastia was characterized by smaller insults. Most kids would just ask, "Why don't you wear a bra?" Even adults could be cruel. "Are you a boy or a girl?" I was often asked.

When wearing shirts, it was crucial that they be loose fitting. If a T-shirt had shrunk in the dryer, I would spend hours and days stretching it out so that it didn't cling to my body. You can see fat boys do this every day.

As a fat kid, and one who hated competition, I learned to loathe sports, especially physical education. The one form of exercise I enjoyed from childhood was swimming. Unfortunately, as my breasts grew, so did my shame about removing my shirt. At summer camp, I never set foot in the swimming pool. I knew that taking off my shirt would bring ridicule, and that leaving it on while swimming would show that I felt ashamed of my body. So, I pretended that I was above swimming—too cool for the pool.

By high school, I had developed remarkable powers of verbal self-defense. I absorbed cruelty and learned how to mete it back out in sharp doses. There's no doubt that this shaped the person I became, for better and for worse. In high school, I managed to carve out a social niche.... The bullying stopped. But the shirts stayed loose-fitting. I rarely went swimming.

The doctors thought perhaps I suffered from low testosterone. I found this funny, since my sex drive had been in high gear since I was a sophomore. Finally, the doctors said that my excess breast tissue was probably just a result of being fat. Lose the weight and the breasts will go away.

So I lost weight. I don't remember how much, but by senior year, I was slender. Girls were starting to talk to me. I was more confident. And I still had breasts. After graduation, the doctors congratulated me on my thin body. Now it was time to get rid of my breasts.

In the first surgery, I was placed under general anesthesia. The doctor made a half moon incision under each nipple and cut out the excess breast tissue, finishing the job with some liposuction. Unfortunately the surgery wasn't a complete success. My breasts were smaller, but lumpy, and my nipples were puckered. It took a second surgery to make everything look "normal."

I was nineteen. On New Year's Eve, I went to a party and got drunk for the first time in my life. There, I met a girl who took my virginity. She was too drunk to insist on taking my shirt off. This was a relief, because under my shirt was a sports bra, and under that, layers of gauze. My chest was still healing from the second surgery. In many senses of the word, I was still becoming a man.

I was reminded of this recently, oddly enough, after reading one of those "humorous" snarky news stories that pop up in the right column of *The Huffington Post*. Perhaps you've seen the photo making the rounds. It's of Barney Frank's "moobs."

The photo inspired similar stories at gay culture site *Queerty,* *Gawker,* and *Slate,* which used the incident as the pretense for a scientific column.

While all of these nominally liberal sites pay lip service to the dignity of gay and transgender people, they miss one thing that is very clear to me. Aside from the obvious fat shaming in these stories, the fixation on "man boobs" reveals our culture's obsession with binary gender. As I noted on *The Huffington Post*'s comment thread before a moderator whisked my comment away, "The only breasts *The Huffington Post* approves of are those of thin, white female celebrities." One of the many comments *HuffPo* didn't delete: "Those boobs would be popular in prison where he belongs."

It's culturally ubiquitous. PETA, for example, is a habitual offender, with ads showing men with larger breasts and the tagline: "Dude Looks Like a Lady? Lose the Breasts. Go Vegetarian."

Men are supposed to have flat chests, hairy bodies, and big penises. Women are supposed to have large breasts, thin, hairless bodies, and tidy labia. Of course, our bodies don't always cooperate and, in fact, we have all the evidence we need that biological sex and gender are not as rigid or fixed as we imagine. There are people who are intersex. There are transgender people and genderqueer people. There are millions of men and boys like me, who also have large breasts, or gynecomastia, a medically harmless (though socially lethal) condition that your insurance just might pay to correct. The prevalence of gynecomastia in adolescent boys is estimated to be as low as 4% and as high as 69%. As one article notes, *"These differences probably result from variations in what is perceived to be normal."* You think?

We're so entrenched in that snips 'n snails bullshit that we can't accept bodies that don't fall on either extreme of the gender continuum. Transgender men and women encounter these attitudes in direct, sometimes life-threatening ways. And, given the misogyny that pervades our society, these pressures are even harder for women and girls, whether they're cisgender or transgender. Their bodies are hated and desired in equal measure. When my bully grabbed my breasts and called me "Tits," he was taking what he wanted. He was also reminding me that I was no better than a girl. . . .

[Today] we live in an age of crowdsourced bullying. I cannot imagine what it would be like to grow up as a boy with breasts today. I suppose I'd spend hours in Photoshop, digitally sculpting my body to remove fat from my face, belly, and chest before uploading my profile photos. If I were a fat girl, I might become very skilled at using light and angles to disguise my less than ideal body, to avoid being dubbed a "SIF" ("secret Internet fatty") by my tech-savvy peers. I would probably become vigilant about removing [Facebook] tags from unflattering photos.

Twenty years have gone by, and I miss my breasts. As a chubby adult male, I still have a small set of breasts, but not the ones I was born with. The two surgeries deprived my nipples of their sensitivity.

I've often joked that if I knew I was going to become a performance artist, I would have kept my breasts. The breasts I have now are smaller but still capable of stoking the body police. I once scandalized a fancy pool party in Las Vegas simply by taking off my shirt. I realize that, as a man, it is my privilege to do so. In most parts of our society, it is either illegal or strongly frowned upon for a woman to go topless. (Female breasts are either for maternity or for male sexual pleasure, not for baring at polite parties.) Perhaps my breasts, which remind people of this prohibition, invite a similar kind of censure.

I've performed naked enough in my adult life to know that the body police can always find a new area to target. I was recently stunned to hear porn actress Dana DeArmond describe me in a podcast interview as a "fat lady" while her host, Joe Rogan, openly theorized that my small penis was somehow connected to my feminism. Rogan's view of gender is so restrictive that he can only conceive of male feminism if it is in a feminized body. (This is probably also why men who support feminism are often dubbed "man-ginas" by misogynists.)

There might actually be tens of thousands of words devoted to describing my fat body and small penis on the Internet. It's almost a point of pride. Now I don't just use my sharp tongue for self-defense. I also use my body itself, as an argument, and as a provocation.

I am Tits. Got a problem with that?

This article originally appeared on My Own Private Guantanamo *on December 21, 2011.*

why breastfeeding
in public is taboo

NICKI LISA COLE

3

Nearly weekly there is a news story about a woman being kicked out of an establishment for breastfeeding her baby. Restaurants, public pools, churches, art museums, courts of law, schools, and stores, including Target, the American Girl Store, and ironically, Victoria's Secret, are all sites of recent skirmishes over a woman's right to nurse.

Breastfeeding *anywhere*, public or private, is a woman's legal right in 47 states.

In South Dakota and Virginia, the right to nurse anywhere is not written in law, but breastfeeding is exempt from laws banning public nudity and indecency. Idaho is the lone state without any laws enforcing a woman's right to nurse. Yet, nursing women are regularly scolded, shamed, given the side-eye, harassed, embarrassed, and made to leave public and private spaces by those who find the practice inappropriate or believe it illegal.

When we consider this problem from the standpoint of rational thought, it makes absolutely no sense. Breastfeeding is a natural, necessary, and healthful part of human life. And, in the United States, for these reasons, it is almost universally protected by law. So why does a cultural taboo on nursing in public exist in our society?

... Let's look for the underlying ideologies of the haters.

One need only examine a handful of accounts of confrontations or online comments to see a pattern. In nearly all cases, the person who asks the woman to leave or harasses her suggests that what she is doing is indecent, scandalous, or lewd. Some do this subtly, by suggesting she "would be more comfortable" if she were hidden from the view of others, or by telling a woman that she must "cover up" or leave. Others are aggressive and overt, like the church official who derogatorily called a mother who nursed during services "a stripper."

Beneath comments like these is the idea that breastfeeding ... is a private act and should be kept as such. From a sociological standpoint, this underlying notion tells us a lot about how people see and understand women and their breasts: as sex objects.

Despite the fact that women's breasts are biologically designed to nourish, they are universally framed as sex objects in our society. This is a frustratingly arbitrary designation based on gender, which becomes clear when one considers that it is illegal for women to bare their breasts (really, their nipples) in public, but men, who also have breast tissue on their chests, are allowed to walk around shirt-free.

We are a society awash in the sexualization of breasts. Their "sex appeal" is used to sell products, to make film and television appealing, and to entice people to men's sporting events, among other things. Because of this, women are often made to feel that they are doing something sexual any time some of their breast tissue is visible. Women with larger breasts, which are hard to comfortably wrangle and cover, know well the stress of trying to hide them from view . . . in an effort to not be harassed or judged as we walk the streets of our communities, as we work, and go to school. In the United States, breasts are always and forever sexual, whether we want them to be or not.

. . . When we sexualize women's bodies, we turn them into sex objects. When women are sex objects, they are meant to be seen, handled, and used for pleasure *at the discretion of men.* They are meant to be passive recipients of sex acts, not agents who decide when and where to make use of their bodies.

Framing women this way denies them subjectivity—the recognition that they are people, not objects—and takes away their rights to self-determination and freedom. Framing women as sex objects is an act of power, and so, too, is shaming women who nurse in public. The real message delivered during these instances of harassment is this: "What you are doing is wrong, you are wrong to insist on doing it, and I am here to stop you."

At the root of this social problem is the belief that women's sexuality is dangerous and bad. Women's sexuality is framed as having the power to corrupt men and boys and make them lose control. . . . It should be hidden from public view and only expressed when invited or coerced by a man.

We, as a society, need to create a welcoming and comfortable climate for nursing mothers. To do so, this doctor recommends the following treatment: Decouple the breast, and women's bodies in general, from sexuality, and stop framing women's sexuality as a problem to be contained.

This article originally appeared on About.com.

gay male athletes and discourses of masculinity

MARKUS GERKE

4

The NBA has its first openly gay player in Jason Collins, and the NFL will follow soon, as former college player Michael Sam is expected to join a team this summer.* This might indicate that we are seeing a radical shift in society's stereotypes about gay men. At the same time, it remains to be seen, as Dave Zirin indicates at *The Nation*, whether gay male athletes can help shift our definitions of masculinity more broadly or whether they might paradoxically reinforce gender norms and notions of hypermasculinity.

In her theory of masculinities, Raewyn Connell identifies four ideal-typical and related versions of masculinity: *hegemonic masculinities* (the cultural ideal of masculinity that legitimizes the superordination of men over women and

Note: This article was published in March 2014.

that most men aspire to), *complicit masculinities* (the majority of men who buy into the hegemonic ideal and who benefit from patriarchy although they are themselves not able to fully embody hegemonic masculinity), *subordinated masculinities* (masculinity's "other," that which is deemed unmanly and culturally connected to femininity), and *marginalized masculinities* (masculinities at the intersection of race and class—men who cannot embody the hegemonic ideal because of their marginalization).

According to Connell, author of *Masculinities*, gay masculinities are the exemplary case of subordinated masculinities: "Gayness, in patriarchal ideology, is the repository of whatever is symbolically expelled from hegemonic masculinity." It is associated with weakness and femininity and thus excluded from what it means to be a "real" man. Based on these cultural stereotypes, it is no wonder that the fact of male gay athletes being visible in the hypermasculine environment of professional sports threatens to destabilize our very notions of masculinity and sexuality.

At the same time, gay male athletes face the challenge of having to navigate or take on these stereotypes after their coming-out. Ironically, it is often hypermasculine discourses that both Michael Sam and Jason Collins drew on when establishing their identities as gay male athletes in public. For instance, Michael Sam is quoted as saying, "If someone calls me a name, I'll have a chat with them. Hopefully it won't lead to anything further"—implying his ability to engage in physical violence to defend himself. And when asked about his reaction to the support he has received from sports fans at his university, he responded, "I wanted to cry, but I'm a man," reinforcing the notion that real men are not supposed to show their emotions (although, one could argue that by admitting that he even had this emotional reaction, he does actually crack open the "manbox" a little bit).

Similarly, in Jason Collins's very thoughtful coming-out article, he repeatedly emphasized his masculine traits of fearlessness, strength, and toughness in trying to call into question stereotypes about gay men:

On the court I graciously accept one label sometimes bestowed on me: "the pro's pro." I got that handle because of my fearlessness and my commitment to my teammates. I take charges and I foul—that's been my forte. [. . .] I'm not afraid to take on any opponent. I love playing against the best. Though Shaquille O'Neal is a Hall of Famer, I never shirked from the challenge of trying to frustrate the heck out of him. (Note to Shaq: My flopping has nothing to do with being gay.) My mouthpiece is in, and my wrists are taped. Go ahead, take a swing—I'll get up. I hate to say it, and I'm not proud of it, but I once fouled a player so hard that he had to leave the arena on a stretcher. I go against the gay stereotype, which is why I think a lot of players will be shocked: *That* guy is gay?

... Do gay male athletes disprove stereotypes about masculinity? Or do they merely prove that gay men can embody hegemonic masculinity?*

On a theoretical level, the transformations we have witnessed over the past few years (from openly gay male athletes to marriage equality) may indicate a shift in Connell's system of masculinities. It seems that gay masculinities are taking on some aspects that defined marginalized masculinities in her theory: Connell pointed out that one of the central factors of marginalized masculinities ... is the inability of these men—as a group—[to gain] legitimacy. Yet, individual marginal men (those deemed exceptional or exemplary) can, in fact, rise to the top and can be considered to embody the masculine ideal. For instance, black actors and athletes (think Michael Jordan) ... can be celebrated as *de facto* hegemonic men despite their racial marginalization. Crucially, though, the rise of these individual men of color

It is crucially important to reiterate Dave Zirin's point that we can't ask Jason Collins or Michael Sam to radically change masculinity for us.... Being a gay male professional athlete today in itself is "a radical act."

does not uplift all men of color into legitimacy; instead, they are still trapped in marginality.

We might be seeing the rise of a few "exceptional" gay men in the world of sports, able to dissociate themselves from the stereotypes surrounding subordinated (i.e., gay) masculinities. However, it remains to be seen whether this will result in stereotypes surrounding gay men being shattered more broadly, or whether society will regard them as merely "exceptional" gay men. And even if we are witnessing a shift away from the association of male homosexuality with weakness, will this result in the destruction of our rigid definitions of masculinity (and femininity)? Or are we instead simply seeing hegemonic masculinity go through a process of modernization, allowing for a greater number of men (including gay men) to assume positions of complicit masculinity, while leaving the overall superordination of men over women intact?

This article originally appeared on Sociological Lens *on March 5, 2014.*

feminizing women's sports teams

GWEN SHARP

I n the book *Strong Women, Deep Closets: Lesbians and Homophobia in Sports,* Pat Griffin discusses the pressure on female athletes to constantly prove they, and their sport, are acceptably feminine, for fear of being labeled lesbians. Women who engage in and openly enjoy sports have often been viewed with suspicion or concern, ranging from beliefs that physical exertion might make them infertile to a fear that women's sports teams serve as recruiting sites for lesbians. Some college coaches even try to recruit young women by hinting to their parents that other schools their daughter is considering are known for having a lot of lesbians and might not be the "type of environment" where they want their sweet little girl to go.

Female athletes and women's sports teams thus often feel a lot of pressure to prove their heterosexuality. One way to do so is to dissociate themselves from lesbians.

Another is to emphasize the femininity of female athletes, signaling that despite their athletic abilities, they are still physically attractive to, and interested in, men.

The Florida State University women's basketball website made me think of Griffin's work. The "Meet the Team" segment of the website includes images of the women dressed in formal dresses, with makeup and hair done, posing in or on limos. Similarly, Texas A&M's promotional media guide features an image of the male coach surrounded by the team members wearing sexy clothing.

While these types of materials have traditionally been for the media, they're increasingly used as recruiting tools for players. [The universities] argue that they're just trying to put out something distinctive to set them apart. And as Jayda Evans at the *Seattle Times* says, it's not like men's sports teams are never photographed off the court.

But when men's teams are dressed up for publicity materials, it's usually for one or two images, outnumbered by those that highlight their sports participation. For female athletes, images that exclude any connection to sports often become nearly the entire story. And despite the fact that the creators often stress their interest in doing something unique and distinctive, there is a common set of elements in promotional materials for women's sports: clothing, makeup, hairstyles, and poses that sexualize the players and implicitly include a reassurance to parents, potential players, and fans that the women are pretty, charming, and feminine, regardless of what they do on the court or the field. That is, the athletes are blending masculinity and femininity by being athletic *and* pretty, not giving up their femininity altogether.

Of course, part of an acceptable performance of femininity is showing that you want male attention, and that you actively try to make yourself appealing to men. So while these materials might do many other things, they also carry a particular message: these girls like to pretty themselves up, and that should reassure you that it's not a team full of lesbians.

The effect is that female athletes may feel pressured to keep their hair long, wear makeup even on the court, and emphasize any relationships they have with men or children to "prove" they are straight, and a lesbian who likes makeup and sexy clothing may face less suspicion and stigma than a straight woman who doesn't.

This article originally appeared on Sociological Images *on December 29, 2009.*

part 2: performances

Who farts? And who cares?

Sociologists Martin Weinberg and Colin Williams wanted to know, so their team interviewed 172 college students about their habits and concerns about farting and pooping. In their article "Fecal Matters," they reported that everybody farts and everybody cares, but not everyone cares all the time or equally.

Over half of heterosexual women worried that someone who overheard their flatulence or defecation would be disgusted. They especially worried that men would overhear them and think that they were unattractive or unladylike. In contrast, about three-quarters of heterosexual men were unconcerned about offending others and didn't worry about the possibility that overhearing such sounds would cause a woman not to like them. "For guys it's kind of like a joke," said one. Almost a quarter of men said that they "often engaged in intentional flatulence," whereas only 7% of women admitted to doing so. "Guys would say it's raunchy and then say 'Nice one,'" explained one guy, "because if it's strong it's more manly." Women felt like they were violating gender norms if their farts were stinky: "The worse it stinks," said one, "the nastier they think I am."

Partly because of these concerns, over three-quarters of women said they felt uncomfortable in public restrooms, compared to only half of men. "In a public restroom," said one woman, "I might try to choose [a bathroom] that I'm fairly certain will be empty, but if I'm feeling particularly paranoid I might wait until someone flushes." Women were also more likely than men to do things to reduce the likelihood that others would detect their bathroom activities, like going into another room to pass gas or letting their stool out slowly to avoid a *kerplunk*.

Two-thirds said they would wait until they were alone to poop, compared to a third of men, and only women reported flushing repeatedly to ensure that the sights and smells of their defecation had disappeared. One of the men said that the only thing he was willing to do to protect others from his bathroom activities was close the door.

Caring about such things was so gendered that men who tried to hide their fecal sounds could be mocked for acting girly.

We had a guy who lived with us two years ago, and he went to great lengths for people not to hear . . . him. He would run the water so we couldn't hear him. He went to extreme lengths. But since we'd hear the water running, we knew what he was doing. We were like: "He's worse than a girl."

Both men and women said they were more concerned about detection if someone they were sexually attracted to was present. "It's unappealing for a man to hear a strange woman poop," said one woman. Another agreed: "I guess it would go back to the whole [idea of] women having to be the attractive one. Like, women wear the makeup, wear the dresses, and are the sex objects." A man admitted that he reluctantly changed his behavior around women: "I'm a guy and I'm a pig, and a lot of girls don't like that," he said, "so I try to control myself a bit."

———

This study is a great example of what social scientists call *doing gender*—modifying our behavior to conform to gendered expectations. We do gender according to gender rules, or instructions for how to appear and behave as a man or woman. Generally, women are expected to have better control of their bodies, to be more polite, and to avoid offending others. All of these things are consistent with being more discreet with farts and poops.

The idea of gender as something that we *do* challenges the belief that gender is something that we *are*. If gender was a singular and fixed trait, women would be more likely than men to try to fart quietly, no matter where they were or who was around. In private, though, there is no incentive for women to control their bodies, so they probably don't. Conversely, if gender was something that we were, men who fart for fun on the couch with their buddies would also do so in job interviews and on first dates, but we know they generally do not.

When we all do gender, even if we don't do it perfectly or all the time, the gender binary can seem more real than it actually is. Everybody farts, but boys and men are more comfortable doing so publicly than girls and women. As a result, one couldn't be blamed for concluding that men, in fact, are smellier and poopier.

In the next few essays, you'll encounter examples of people doing gender: a woman who transforms her look from masculine to feminine, a study of the gendered use of a verbal tic, the importance of our clothes and accessories, and the way that our choice of partner—or partners—shapes the range of gender we're allowed to exhibit.

—LISA WADE

masculinity, gender (non)conformity, and queer visibility

TRISTAN BRIDGES AND C.J. PASCOE

Coco Layne got a haircut. She shaved both sides of her head but left the top at a length that falls roughly to the bottom of her face. As a feminist fashion, art, and lifestyle blogger, she was quick to recognize the ways that she could subtly re-style her hair and dramatically alter her presentation of gender. So, in classic feminist art blogger style, she produced an art project depicting her experience....

Coco's "Warpaint" is a critical commentary on what gender is, where it comes from, how flexible it is, what this flexibility means, and what gender (non)conformity has to do with sexuality. Coco's work provides important lessons about how gender is produced just below the radar of most people most of the time. Projects like this point out the extensive work that goes into *doing gender* in a way that is recognizable by others.

Indeed, recognition by others is key to doing gender "correctly." It is what scholar Judith Butler calls *performativity*, or the way in which people are compelled to engage in an identifiably gendered performance. When people fail to do this, Butler argues that they are *abject*—not culturally decipherable—and thus subject to all sorts of social sanctions.

Butler points out that the performance of gender itself produces a belief that something, someone, or some authentic, inalienable gendered self lies behind the performance. ["Warpaint"] lays bare the fiction that there is this sort of inevitably gendered self behind the performance of gender. This is precisely why projects like this produce such discussion and, for some, discomfort. It makes (some of) us uncomfortable by challenging our investments in and folk theories surrounding certain ways of thinking about gender and sexuality.

Much of the commentary on the "Warpaint" project focused on Coco's ability to get a retail job when she displayed her body in [the most "feminine" ways]. Her experience reflects research indicating that different workplaces reward particular gender appearances and practices. Kristen Schilt's research on trans men at work, for instance, highlights the way that performances of masculinity get translated into workplace acceptance for these men.

Yet doing gender in a way that calls into question its naturalness can put people (including those who do not identify as genderqueer or trans) at risk. In *Jespersen v. Harrah*, the 9th Circuit Court of Appeals held that female employees can be required to wear makeup as a condition of employment (in a workplace where men are not required to wear it). While recent decisions have been more favorable to trans-identified employees, most states do not have employment law or school policies protecting gender-nonconforming individuals. Simply put, most states do not have laws addressing—to use Coco's language—gender expression.

For Coco, however, "Warpaint" is also about queer visibility. Coco identifies as a queer femme woman. On a typical day, she claims to fall somewhere on the third or fourth row of her set of images [that is, closer to a "feminine" self-presentation]. She artistically explores the ways that subtle changes in hairstyle, makeup, and clothing cause dramatic transformations in how others perceive her. And while Coco's more "femme" presentations helped her get a job, she also discusses the ways that those same presentations of her body worked against queer visibility. As Coco put it: "I struggle with femme visibility and find it a little challenging to have the queer community recognize me to be 'as queer as they are' because of how femme I look sometimes."

While gender identity and performance and sexual identity are not the same, gendered practices and presentations also signal membership in sexual communities, as Coco points out. Often, gender nonconformity is socially interpreted as a declaration of gay identity. Conversely, gender conformity is often "read" as straight. So, gender-conforming gay men and women and gender-nonconforming straight men and women might struggle with visibility. Mignon Moore's research on black lesbian communities addresses a similar set of struggles: Moore finds that the gender performances of the women she studied were strongly associated with sexual desires as her participants discussed finding gender expressions that elicited recognition and attention from desired audiences. Moore's research is concerned with spaces where queer recognition is desired and provides status and a sense of community and belonging. However, queer visibility—as Coco's experience looking for work attests—affords a different set of consequences in different kinds of contexts.

As Coco highlights, the movement between masculinity and femininity, as well as the gray area in between, can be accomplished regardless of the sex of one's body. The story of "Warpaint" is not just artistic; it is also about the way that gendered performances signify belonging to (or being excluded from) a community.

This article originally appeared on Girl w/ Pen! *on December 4, 2014.*

what is "winning women talk more like a girl (on *jeopardy!*)"?

VIRGINIA RUTTER

What's the big deal about uptalk? The College of William & Mary's Tom Linneman took a look at how women and men both use uptalk in his new study "Gender in *Jeopardy!* Intonation Variation on a Television Game Show" in *Gender & Society*. The punchline: Women use uptalk more frequently, but men use it as well. For men, however, uptalk signals something *completely different*.

What is uptalk? "Uptalk is the use of a rising, questioning intonation when making a statement, which has become quite prevalent in contemporary American speech," explains Linneman. Uptalk in the United States is reported to have emerged in the 1980s among adolescent women in California, aka "Valley Girls," and it has become more widely used by men and women since then. Uptalk has been associated with a way of talking that makes women sound less confident.

Jeopardy! was Linneman's clever setting for observing how women and men use the speech pattern. The sociologist analyzed the use of uptalk by carefully coding 5,500 responses from 300 contestants in 100 episodes of the popular game show. He looked at what happened to speech patterns when contestants from a variety of backgrounds gave their answers.

Although the contestants were asked to phrase their responses in the form of a question, they used uptalk just over a third of the time.

Linneman found that men use uptalk as a way to signal uncertainty. Linneman explained, "On average, women used uptalk nearly twice as often as men. However, if men responded incorrectly, their intonation betrayed their uncertainty: Their use of uptalk shot up dramatically." On average, men who answered correctly used uptalk only 27% of the time. Among incorrect responses, men used uptalk 57% of the time. In contrast, a woman who answered correctly used uptalk 48% of the time, nearly as often as an incorrect man."

Men's uptalk increased when they were less confident, and also when they were correcting women—but not men. When a man corrected another man—that is, following a

Probability of Uptalk by Certainty, Age, Race, and Gender

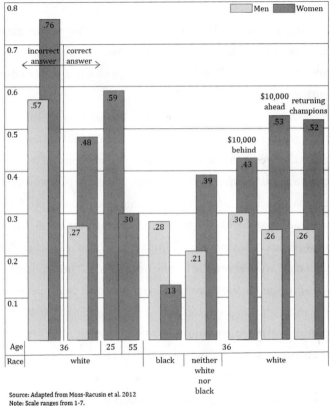

Source: Adapted from Moss-Racusin et al. 2012
Note: Scale ranges from 1-7.
Graphic created for TheSocietyPages.org by Suzy McElrath

FIGURE 1: Illustrative predicted probabilities of uptalk
Note: Predictions calculated using logistic coefficients from Table 2,
Model B and the following formula: $p = e^2/(1 + e^2)$. All examples, unless
otherwise noted, are challengers (i.e., not returning champions) who
are neither ahead nor behind.

man's incorrect answer with a correct one—he used uptalk 22% of the time. When a man corrected a woman, though, he used uptalk 53% of the time. Linneman speculates that men are engaging in a kind of chivalry: men can be blunt with another man in public, but feel obliged to use a softer edge with a woman.

And how do women use uptalk? As Linneman explains, "One of the most interesting findings coming out of the project is that success has an opposite effect on men and women on the show." Linneman measured success in two ways: He compared challengers to returning champions, and he tracked how far ahead or behind contestants were when they responded. Linneman found that, "The more successful a man is on the show, the *less* he uses uptalk. The opposite is true for women: the more successful a woman is on the show, the *more* she uses uptalk." Linneman suspects that this is "because women continute to feel they must apologize for their success."

This article originally appeared on Girl w/ Pen! *on February 8, 2013.*

the balancing act of being female

LISA WADE

osea Lake posted the image on the following page to her Tumblr, and it struck a chord. What I like about the image is the way it very clearly illustrates two things. First, it reveals that doing femininity doesn't mean obeying a single, simple rule. Instead, it's about occupying and traveling within a certain space. In this case, usually between "proper" and "flirty." Women have to constantly figure out where in that space they're supposed to be. Too flirty at work means you won't be taken seriously; too proper at the bar and you're invisible. Under the right circumstances (e.g., Halloween, a funeral), you can do "cheeky" or "old fashioned."

The second thing I like about this image is the way it shows that there is a significant price to pay for getting it wrong. It's not just a *faux pas*. Once you're "asking for it," you could be a target. And once you've reached "prudish," you've

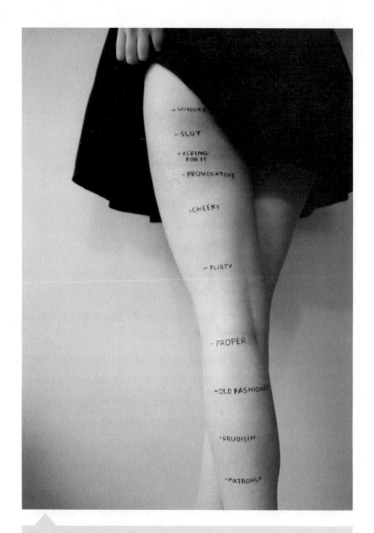

© Rosea Lake, used with permission.

become socially irrelevant. Both violence and social marginalization are serious consequences.

And, of course, all women are going to get it wrong sometimes because the boundaries are moving targets. What's cheeky in one setting or to one person is flirty in or to another. So women constantly risk getting it wrong, or getting it wrong to someone. The consequences are always floating out there, worrying us, and sending us to the mall.

Indeed, this is why women have so many clothes. We need an all-purpose black skirt that does old-fashioned, another one to do proper, and a third to do flirty—at the very least—and all in casual, business, and formal. And we need heels to go with each (stilettos = provocative, high heels = flirty, low heels = proper, etc., plus we need flats for the picnics and beach weddings). And we need pants that are hemmed to the right length for each of these pairs of shoes. You can't wear black shoes with navy pants, so you'll need to double up on all these things if you want any color variety in your wardrobe. I could go on, but you get the picture.

Women's closets are often mocked as a form of self-indulgence, shopaholic-ism, or narcissism. But this isn't fair. Instead, if a woman is class-privileged enough, her closet reflects an (often unarticulated) understanding of just how complicated the rules are. If she's not class-privileged enough, she can't follow the rules and is punished for being, for example, "trashy" or "unprofessional." It's a difficult job that we impose on women, and we're all too often damned if we do and damned if we don't.

This article originally appeared on Sociological Images *on January 22, 2013.*

doing gender with
wallets and purses

TRISTAN BRIDGES

once heard a transgender woman give a talk about the process of socially transitioning to being recognized as a woman. She discussed various decisions she made in taking some final, critical steps toward the social identity of a woman. . . . But what struck me the most was her discussion of carrying a purse.

. . . If asked what I thought would be a significant everyday challenge if I were a woman, I don't think "purse" would have been high on my list. But she discussed remembering to bring it, how to carry it, norms surrounding purse protection in public, but also more intimate details like what *belongs* in a purse.

Purses and wallets are gendered spaces. There's nothing inherent in men's and women's constitutions that naturally recommends carrying money and belongings in different containers. Like the use of urinals in men's restrooms, wallets and purses are a way of producing understandings of gender difference rather than a natural consequence of differences.

In Christena Nippert-Eng's book *Islands of Privacy,* a sociological study of privacy in everyday life, one chapter deals specifically with wallets and purses. She used participants' wallets and purses as a means of getting them to think more critically about privacy. Participants were asked to empty the contents of their wallets and purses and to form two piles with the contents: "more private" and "more public." As they sifted through the contents, they talked about why they carried what they carried as well as how and why they thought about it as public or private.

After collecting responses, Nippert-Eng documented all of the contents and created categories and distinctions between objects based on how people thought about them as public or private. Invariably, objects defined as more personally meaningful were also considered more private. Another [distinction] that routinely arose was how damaging it might be for participants if a specific object was taken.

Based on these findings, she creates a useful table delineating participants' concerns surrounding and understandings of the objects they carry with them (see the following page).

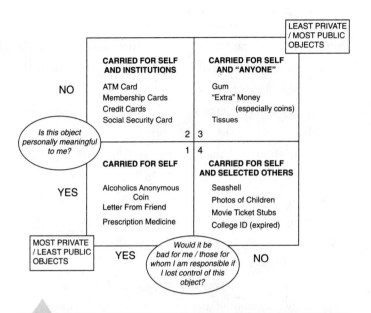

There's sort of a sliding scale of privacy from most to least private as one proceeds from the bottom left cell to the top right cell. Thus, items classified by participants in the lower left cell (1) are the most private objects—things like prescription medications [and] letters from friends.

Other items were still considered private, but "less private" than objects in cell 1 because they were shared selectively. While credit cards, bank cards, memberships, and money were all classified as "private," individuals also thought of them as "more public" than objects in cell 1 because they were required to share these objects with institutions throughout their lives.

Similarly, some objects were thought of as "private," but were also carried to share with certain others, such as photographs of children. Finally, items classified in the top right cell are the most public objects in wallets and purses—carried for the self and, potentially, "anyone" else. Items here include things like tissues, lip balm, money classified as "extra," gum, breath mints, etc.

Objects from most of the cells exist in both wallets and purses, but not all of them. The "most public" objects are inequitably distributed between wallets and purses. As Nippert-Eng writes, "This is the one category of objects that is overwhelmingly absent for participants who carry only wallets, yet universally present for those who carry purses." . . . "Wallet carriers" in her sample carry only objects necessary for institutional transactions.

This is, I believe, a wonderful analysis of one of the more subtle ways in which gender is accomplished in daily life. Certain objects are simply more likely to be carried in purses. Interestingly, this class of "feminine" objects is also [comprised of] objects that play a critical role in social interactions. Indeed, many of us are able to travel without these objects because we can "count on" purse-carriers to have them. It's an aspect of care work by which some (those carrying purses) care for others (those without purses). And if they're any good at it, the caring goes virtually unacknowledged, [unless] these objects are absent. Indeed, these objects may be carried in anticipation of others' requests. It's a small aspect of doing gender, but a significant element of social interactions and life.

When I was learning about interviewing and ethnography, I was told to always carry a pack of gum, a pack of cigarettes (something "lite"), and a lighter. My professor told me, "It opens people up. It's a small gesture that comforts people—puts them at ease." These are the ways you might want people to feel if you're asking them to "open up" for you. I still remember my first foray into "the field." I bought my gum and cigarettes (objects I don't typically carry) and the first thought I had was, "Where the heck am I going to keep these things?" What I didn't realize at the time was that I was asking an intensely gendered question.

This article originally appeared on Sociological Images *on November 13, 2013.*

compulsory monogamy in *the hunger games*

MIMI SCHIPPERS

NPR's Linda Holmes wrote a great article about the gender dynamics in *The Hunger Games: Catching Fire* and concluded, "You could argue that Katniss' conflict between Peeta and Gale is effectively a choice between a traditional Movie Girlfriend and a traditional Movie Boyfriend." I do love the way Holmes puts this. Gender, it seems, is not what one is, but what one does. Different characteristics we associate with masculinity and femininity are available to everyone, and when Peeta embodies some characteristics we usually see only in women's roles, Peeta becomes the Movie Girlfriend despite being a boy.

Though I find this compelling, I want to take a moment to focus on the other part of this sentence—the part when Holmes frames Katniss' relationship to Peeta and Gale as a "conflict between" and a "choice." I think that, in some ways, the requirement to choose one or the other forces Katniss to not only "choose" a boyfriend, but also to choose gender.

Depending on whether she's relating to Peeta or Gale, she is either someone who takes charge, is competent in survival, and protects her partner (traditionally the masculine role) or someone who lets another lead and nurtures instead of protects (the feminine role). As Candace West and Don Zimmerman suggested many years ago in their article "Doing Gender," we do gender in relationship to other people. It's a conversation or volley in which we're expected to play the part to the way others are doing gender.

When Katniss is with Peeta, she does a form of masculinity in relationship and reaction to his behavior and vice versa. Because Peeta "calls out" protection, Katniss steps up. When Gale calls out nurturing, she plays the part. In other words, not only is gender a "doing" rather than a "being," it is also an interactive process. Because Katniss exists in relation to both Peeta and Gale, and because each embodies and calls out different ways of doing gender, Katniss oscillates between being the "movie boyfriend" sometimes and the "movie girlfriend" other times and, it seems, she's facile and takes pleasure in doing all of it. If Katniss has to "choose" Peeta or Gale, she will have to give up doing gender in this splendid and, dare I say, feminist and queer way.

Now imagine a world in which Katniss wouldn't have to choose.

What if she could be in a relationship with Peeta [and fulfill her need to be] understood, nurtured, and protective, while also getting her girl on with Gale? In other words, imagine a world without compulsory monogamy, where having two or more boyfriends or girlfriends was possible.

I'm currently working on *Beyond Monogamy: Polyamory and the Future of Polyqueer Sexualities*, a book on monogamy and the queer potential for open and polyamorous relationships. I'm writing about the ways in which compulsory monogamy fits nicely into and perpetuates cultural ideas about masculinity and femininity and how different forms of non-monogamy might open up alternative ways of doing not just relationships, but also gender.

Forcing Katniss to choose is forcing Katniss into monogamy and into doing gender to complement her partner. Victoria Robinson points out in her article "My Baby Just Cares for Me" that monogamy compels women to invest too much time, energy, and resources into an individual man and limits their autonomy and relationships with others. What Robinson doesn't talk about is how it also limits women's range of how they might do gender in relationship to others.

[Monogamy] also limits men's range of doing gender in relationships. Wouldn't it be nice if Peeta and Gale never felt the pressure to be something they are not? Imagine how Peeta's and Gale's masculinities would have to be reconfigured to accommodate and accept each other.

Elisabeth Sheff, in her groundbreaking research on polyamorous people, found that both women and men in polyamorous relationships say that the men have to rethink their masculinities to be less possessive, and women have room to be more assertive about their needs and desires.

What this suggests is that monogamy doesn't just limit *who* you can do; it also limits *what* you can do in terms of gender. Might I suggest that Katniss is such a well-rounded woman character precisely because she is polyamorous? ... She's strong, vulnerable, capable, nurturing, and loyal, and we get to see all of it because she does gender differently with her boyfriends. ...

I don't know how her story ends, but I for one am hoping that if there is a happily-ever-after for Katniss, it's not because girl gets boy; it's because girl gets both boys.

This post originally appeared on Marx in Drag *on December 2, 2013.*

high heels
and distinction
among women

LISA WADE

don't know about other women, but whenever I go shopping for shoes, I'm always stunned by the incredible disproportion of high heels. I'm just gonna guesstimate here, but I'll bet 85% of the shoes at the average store are high heels, many so impractical that most women only wear them on special occasions that involve a lot of sitting down. These shoes, moreover, seem to be pushed to the front of the display. Women's shoe stores beckon shoppers by putting their most outrageous shoes out front. You have to go digging for a practical pump.

How is it that a shoe that gets 1% of feet time takes up so much retail space?

Elsewhere, I've reviewed the history of the high heel. Originally a shoe for high-status men, it was soon adopted by the lower classes. Elites responded by heightening the heel. The higher the heel, the more impractical the shoe. Eventually the working classes couldn't keep up with the escalation because they had to, you know, work. Sociologically, this is an example of what Pierre Bourdieu famously called "distinction." The rich work to preserve certain cultural arenas and products for themselves. This allows them to signify their status and avoid getting confused with the masses.

Today, certain class advantages make it easier for upper-middle-class and wealthy women to don high heels. High heels can really only be worn routinely by women who don't work on their feet all day (I'll grant there are dedicated exceptions). Valet parking makes it a whole lot easier to wear shoes that hurt to walk in; so does not having to take the bus. Having money in itself means that nothing stands between you and buying things that are impractical. This, I think, is why the highest, spikiest heels are at the front of the shoe store. In a certain way, they signify status. Wearing those shoes promises to differentiate you from other, "lesser" women, women who can't invest in their appearance and get lots of practice looking elegant on their tip toes.

Women of all classes desire such shoes because of the signals they send. They often buy them aspirationally, hoping to be the type of woman who wears them. It's primarily women at the top of the class hierarchy who will be able to wear them routinely, though, feeding the supply of barely worn spike heels that populate every thrift store in America. So that's my theory.

But let's complicate it just a bit more. Since working-class people do, ultimately, have access to high-heeled shoes, the upper classes have to go to extra lengths to effectively use high heels as a marker of distinction. This can be accomplished by sub-dividing high heels into "classy" and "trashy." [Do a Google Images search for "stripper shoes," then pull up images of some Louis Vuitton heels.]

Now I know that you can get "classy" heels for much less money than a pair of Louis Vuitton heels, but the point is to identify this as an arms race. The rich have the power to control the discourse and can always access the high-status objects. The poor can copy, but they are often playing catch-up because the rich are always changing the rules. So, as soon as the poor are doing it right, the rules change. Otherwise the activity or item doesn't function to distinguish the rich from the poor. And so on.

This post originally appeared on Sociological Images *on February 25, 2013.*

part 3: inequalities

Somewhere around 16 years old, when it's typical for girls growing up in America to begin babysitting, I worked for a neighbor with quadruplets. I usually kept a pretty good handle on things . . . until bedtime. Here's how it went one night:

I delivered a kind but stern talking to about going to bed on time and marched all four girls to their shared bedroom. After pushing four heads through pajama tops and sixteen limbs through pajama tops and bottoms, I got them all into bed.

Then it began.

Julia leapt out of bed and ran into the kitchen to get a glass of water. I followed her to help. While I was away, Tina got up to go to the bathroom. As I brought Julia back to bed, Jennifer decided she was thirsty, too. Back to the kitchen.

In the meantime, Cathy wandered off to an unknown corner of the house. Tina called for help in the bathroom. Abandoning the kitchen, I rushed in to avert disaster. Bringing her back to the bedroom, I realized Cathy and Jennifer were still missing. I found Julia in the kitchen, eating peanut butter out of a jar with her fingers. I swiped the jar, screwed on the lid, and put it on top of the refrigerator. I pointed her to the bedroom and went to look for Cathy, the one whose location was a mystery. I found her in her parents' bedroom digging through her mother's jewelry box. "No, it's bedtime," my 16-year-old self said as authoritatively as I could muster, pulling gold links through her fingers and stuffing them back in the box. I hoisted her onto my hip and walked back toward her bedroom.

As I turned the corner, I found Julia and Tina climbing the walls, literally. They were practicing the time-honored child tradition of straddling the hallway with their arms and legs and ascending the walls like human spiders. I put Cathy down, who went screaming underneath their legs past her bedroom and into the kitchen, trying to pull down the wall climbers. In the meantime, the other—I can't remember now which one it was—had pulled a dining room chair to the refrigerator and was teetering on top of it as she stretched her hand toward the forbidden jar of peanut butter.

There were exactly zero children in bed.

Babysitting is hard and, according to a 2014 study by Robin Dhar, 97% of babysitters are female. It's almost all female at the professional level, too. A whopping 96% of child care workers are female. It is one of the most gender-segregated jobs in the United States.

In general, women do more of the care-intensive work of society than men do (both the kind that gets paid and the kind done for free). That means that women do more direct caregiving of children, the disabled, and the elderly, and they do more of the housework that enables families to be safe, clean, fed, and happy.

As this example suggests, it starts when we're kids. Research projects on children's time use find that boys do 43 to 46 minutes of chores for every hour that girls do. When asked to list the chores they do, girls list 42% more than boys. Girls are as likely as boys to participate in outside chores and more likely to clean their own rooms, help prepare meals, and care for siblings and pets; the only thing boys report doing more often than girls is basic housecleaning. The University of Michigan's Institute for Social Research concludes girls spend more time on chores than they do playing; the opposite is true for boys.

Not only are girls more likely to be asked to help out around the house, they are less likely to get paid. Boys are 15% more likely than girls to get an allowance for the chores they do. And when girls do get paid, they get a lower wage than their brothers. Likewise, male babysitters get paid

$0.50 more an hour than females. Girls, reports Sweeney Research, do 35% more work than boys but pocket only $0.73 cents on boys' dollar.

Gender in the United States isn't just about difference; it's about inequality. It's about the valuing of men over women, what we call *sexism*; the valuing of masculinity over femininity, what we call *androcentrism*; and the practice of *subordination*, in which women are routinely put in positions that require them to be submissive to or dependent on men.

Child care and housework are all those things. Androcentrism makes us inclined to think that (masculinized) work outside the home is more interesting, valuable, and difficult than (feminized) work inside the home. And when women do more of it, it means they're doing more of men's dirty work than men themselves are doing. That's subordination because it puts women in the position of disproportionately taking care of others' needs. And, insofar as being held responsible for those things translates into fewer hours and opportunities for advancement at work, it makes women dependent on men's higher salaries. That's subordination, too. If it seems natural or comfortable that women sacrifice their own interests and advancement for men by doing more of the devalued work, that's partly because of sexism. If a world that is gender-flipped sounds less fair to you—one where men do more housework and child care so that women can make more money and further their careers—you may have internalized a tinge of sexism. Don't worry, we all have.

Inequality is also about *intersectionality*—the way that gender intersects with all the other things about us: our race, class, age, attractiveness, level of ability, immigration status, sexual orientation, and more—and housework is a good example here, too. Often, the only way for women to pursue careers that allow them to support their families financially is to hire *other* women to do some of the feminized work for them. Housekeepers and nannies who do this work are usually women themselves, and more often than not they are working class or poor, women of color, or immigrant women.

Housework is just one place where we find gender inequality. In this section, we show how gender inequality is part of our daily lives by offering examples from the classroom, our closets, the workplace, the media, and our psyches.

—LISA WADE

beyond bossy or brilliant: gender bias in student evaluations

TRISTAN BRIDGES, KJERSTIN GRUYS, CHRISTIN MUNSCH, AND C.J. PASCOE

Not surprisingly, the new online interactive chart "Gendered Language in Teacher Reviews" has been the subject of a lot of conversation among sociologists, especially those of us who study gender.

We've long known that student evaluations of teaching are biased. A recent experiment made headlines when Adam Driscoll and Andrea Hunt found that professors teaching online received dramatically different evaluation scores depending on whether students thought the professor was a man or a woman; students rated male-identified instructors significantly higher than female-identified instructors, regardless of the instructor's actual gender.

Schmidt's interactive chart provides a bit more information about exactly *what* students are saying when evaluating their professors in gendered ways. Thus far, most commentaries have focused on the fact that men are more likely to be seen as "geniuses," "brilliant," and "funny," while women, as C.J. Pascoe discovered, are more likely to be seen as "bossy," "mean," or "pushy."

These discrepancies are important, but in this post, we've used the tool to shed light on some forms of gendered workplace inequality that have received less attention: comments concerning physical appearance, comments related to messiness and organization, and comments related to emotional (as opposed to intellectual) work performed by professors.

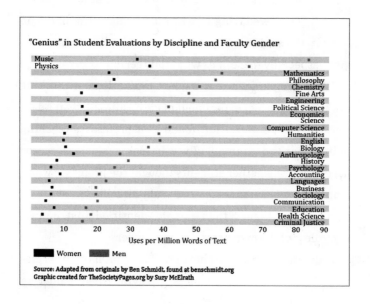

"Genius" in Student Evaluations by Discipline and Faculty Gender

Uses per Million Words of Text

Women   Men

Source: Adapted from originals by Ben Schmidt, found at benschmidt.org
Graphic created for TheSocietyPages.org by Suzy McElrath

physical appearance

The results from Schmidt's chart are not universally "bad" or "worse" for women. For instance, the results for students referring to professors as "hot" and "attractive" are actually mixed. Further, in some fields of study, women are more likely to receive "positive" appearance-based evaluations while, in other fields, men are more likely to receive these evaluations.

A closer examination, however, reveals an interesting pattern. Here is a list of the fields in which *women* are more likely to be referred to as "hot" or "attractive": criminal justice, engineering, political science, business, computer science, physics, economics, and accounting. And here is a list of fields in which *men* are more likely to receive these evaluations: philosophy, English, anthropology, fine arts, languages, and sociology.

Men are sexualized when they teach in fields culturally associated with "femininity" and women are sexualized when they teach in fields culturally associated with "masculinity." Part of this is certainly due to gender segregation in fields of study. There are simply more men in engineering and physics courses. Assuming most students are heterosexual, women teaching in these fields might be more likely to be objectified. Similarly, men teaching in female-dominated fields have a higher likelihood of being evaluated

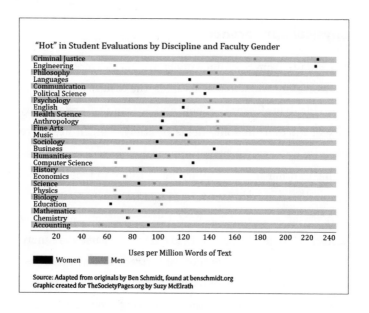

"Hot" in Student Evaluations by Discipline and Faculty Gender

Criminal Justice
Engineering
Philosophy
Languages
Communication
Political Science
Psychology
English
Health Science
Anthropology
Fine Arts
Music
Sociology
Business
Humanities
Computer Science
History
Economics
Science
Physics
Biology
Education
Mathematics
Chemistry
Accounting

20   40   60   80   100   120   140   160   180   200   220   240

Uses per Million Words of Text

■ Women   ▨ Men

Source: Adapted from originals by Ben Schmidt, found at benschmidt.org
Graphic created for TheSocietyPages.org by Suzy McElrath

as "hot" because there are more women there to evaluate them.

Nonetheless, it is important to note that sexual objectification works differently when it's aimed at men. Women, but not men, are systematically sexualized in ways that work to symbolically undermine their authority. (This is why "mothers," "mature," "boss," and "teacher" are among men's top category searches on many online pornography sites.) And women are more harshly criticized for failing to meet normative appearance expectations. Schmidt's chart lends support to this interpretation, as women professors are also almost universally more likely to be referred to as "ugly," "hideous," and "nasty."

level of (dis)organization

Christin Munsch and Kjerstin Gruys are beginning a new research project designed to evaluate whether students assess disorganized or "absent-minded" professors (e.g., messy offices, chalk on their clothing, disheveled appearances) differently depending on gender. Schmidt's interactive chart foreshadows what they might find. Consider the following: women are more likely to be described as "unprepared," "late," and "scattered." These are characteristics we teach little girls to avoid. . . .

In short, we hold men and women to different organizational and self-presentation standards. Consequently, women, but not men, are held accountable when they are perceived to be unprepared or messy. Emphasizing this greater scrutiny of women's organization and professionalism is the finding that women are more likely than men to be described as *either* "professional" *or* "unprofessional," and *either* "organized" *or* "disorganized."

emotional labor

Finally, *emotional* (rather than *intellectual*) terms are used more often in women's evaluations than men's. Whether mean, kind, caring, or rude, students are more likely to comment on these qualities when women are teaching. When women professors receive praise for being "caring," "compassionate," "nice," and "understanding," this is also a not-so-subtle way of telling them that they *should* exhibit these qualities. Thus, men may receive fewer comments related to this type of emotion work because students do not expect them to be doing it in the first place.

There are all sorts of things that are left out of this quick and dirty analysis (race, class, course topic, type of institution, etc.), but it does suggest we begin to question the ways teaching evaluations may systematically advantage some over others. Moreover, if certain groups—for instance, women and scholars of color (and female scholars of color)— are more likely to be in jobs for which teaching evaluations matter more for tenure and promotion, then unfair and biased evaluations may exacerbate inequality within the academy.

This post originally appeared on Girl w/ Pen! *on March 4, 2015.*

13

not seeing is still believing

how visually impaired women understand and experience media representation of the feminine ideal

TARA FANNON

t's known that Western societies are appearance obsessed. Being conventionally attractive, polished, and put-together symbolizes good health and demonstrates control and competence. This has real social advantages for men and women alike. It can mean getting the job you want, the partner you want, the lifestyle you want. Women, we know, are inundated with an ideal of femininity that has, in many ways, become an indicator of self-worth. Although the topic of appearance and the feminine ideal has been thoroughly researched, how visually impaired women manage our appearance-obsessed culture has been left less examined (but see Gili Hammer's work in *Gender & Society*). . . .

Drawing on in-depth interviews and personal diaries with seven Irish women, ages 20–45, all with very little to no sight, I explore how visually impaired women experience mainstream representations of the feminine ideal and to what extent these representations affect their body and self-image.

When asked to describe the media's version of the feminine ideal, the women used words that would be familiar to anyone with sight: fit, lean, thin, good skin, blond, young, nice breasts, and long legs. They agreed that maintaining presentable appearances demonstrated self-respect, command of oneself, and, above all, ability. At the same time, their awareness of being judged based on these same criteria manifested as pressure to be thinner, prettier, younger, and more fashionable. They offset these pressures by engaging in a variety of conventional rituals, such as dieting, exercising, undergoing regular beauty treatments, using cosmetics, and wearing fashionable clothing.

Concurrently, they used adapted sensory strategies to carry out some of these rituals. For example, some relied on voice-activated software to help organize clothing and accessories and create matching outfits (which was very important). Texture was explained to me as a critical way that blind and visually impaired persons have more say in developing and expressing a personal style. The participants used touch and feel to determine aesthetic taste in all things appearance-related, from clothing to cosmetics. The most important strategy was the use of sighted assistance.... All of the women worked closely with a trusted friend or family member whose advice was sought on clothing and accessory purchases. Sighted assistance, in another participant's words, is a way to create a "unique style" but in a "secondhand manner."

Self-assessing, visually comparing, gauging surroundings, and perceiving body language were described as part of looking and feeling confident. Participants emphasized the importance of appearance, but not knowing one's own appearance and being seen by others, while not being able to visually reciprocate, were sources of anxiety that often left them feeling vulnerable and insecure.

According to one participant, "the eyes are used as weapons" to visually scrutinize others; and being blind, according to another participant, "creates an imbalance" in social settings. Such instances were known to test confidence and trigger negative thoughts and feelings. When asked about this, one participant said, "Sometimes I feel disappointed in myself, and think, why can't I do this? Why can't I know? I feel like I'm kind of the problem."

In sum, investing in the body and appearance afforded the participants a sense of power as women and freedom from their disability. Maintaining attractiveness helped to manage a positive self-image and became a way to minimize "difference" and maximize "sameness" among female peers and sighted others.

This article originally appeared on the Gender & Society *blog on November 19, 2013.*

when your (brown) body is a (white) wonderland

TRESSIE MCMILLAN COTTOM

M iley Cyrus made news with a carnival-like stage performance at the 2013 MTV Video Music Awards that included life-size teddy bears, flesh-colored underwear, and plenty of quivering brown buttocks. Almost immediately after the performance, many black women challenged Cyrus's appropriation of black dance ("twerking"). Many white feminists defended Cyrus's right to be a sexual woman without being slut-shamed. Yet others wondered why Cyrus's sad attempt at twerking was news when the United States is planning military action in Syria.

I immediately thought of a summer I spent at UNC Chapel Hill. My partner at the time fancied himself a revolutionary born too late for all the good protests. At a Franklin Street pub one night we were the only black couple at a happy hour. It is one of those college places where concoctions of the bar's finest bottom-shelf liquor are served in huge fishbowls for pennies on the alcohol proof dollar. I saw a few white couples imbibing and beginning some version of bodily grooving to the DJ. I told my partner that one of them would be offering me free liquor and trying to feel my breasts within the hour.

He balked, thinking I was joking.

I then explained to him my long, storied, documented history of being accosted by drunk white men and women in atmospheres just like these. Women asking to feel my breasts in the ladies' restroom. Men asking me for a threesome as their drunk girlfriend or wife looked on smiling. Frat boys offering me cash to "motorboat" my cleavage. Country boys in cowboy hats attempting to impress their buddies by grinding on my ass to an Outkast music set. It's almost legend among my friends who have witnessed it countless times.

My partner could not believe it until, not 30 minutes later, with half the fishbowl gone, a white woman bumped and grinded up to our table and, laughing, told me that her boyfriend would love to see us dance. "C'mon girl! I know you can daaaaannnce," she said. To sweeten the pot they bought our table our own fishbowl.

My partner was stunned. That summer we visited lots of similar happy hours. By the third time this scene played out, my partner had taken to standing guard while I danced, stonily staring down every white couple that looked my way. We were kicked out of a few bars when he challenged some white guy to a fight about it. I hate such scenes, but I gave my partner a break. He was a man and not used to this. He didn't have the vocabulary borne of black breasts that sprouted before bodies had cleared statutory rape guidelines. He didn't know the words, so he did all he knew how to do to tell me he was sorry this was my experience in life: he tried to kick every white guy's ass in Chapel Hill.

. . . What I saw in Cyrus's performance was not just a clueless, culturally insensitive attempt to assert her sexuality or a simple act of cultural appropriation at the expense of black bodies. Instead, I saw what kinds of black bodies were on that stage with Cyrus. Cyrus's dancers looked more like me than they did Rihanna or Beyoncé or Halle Berry. The difference is instructive.

Fat non-normative black female bodies are kith and kin with historical caricatures of black women as work sites, production units, subjects of victimless sexual crimes, and embodied deviance. As I said in my analysis of hip-hop and country music crossovers, playing the desirability of black female bodies as a "wink-wink" joke is a way of lifting up our deviant sexuality without lifting up black women as equally desirable to white women. Cyrus did not just have black women gyrating behind her. She had particularly *rotund* black women.... It's a dance between performing sexual freedom and maintaining a hierarchy of female bodies from which white women benefit materially....

Being desirable is a commodity. Capital and capitalism are gendered systems. The very form that money takes—paper and not goods—is rooted in a historical enterprise of controlling the development of an economic sphere where women might amass wealth. As wealth is a means of power in a capitalistic society, controlling this means of acceptable monies was a way of controlling the accumulation, distribution, and ownership of capital.

For black women, that form of money was embodied by the very nature of how we came to be in America.

Our bodies were literally production units. As living cost centers, we not only produced labor as in work but we produced actual labor through labor; we birthed more cost centers. The legendary "one drop" rule of determining blackness was legally codified not just out of ideological purity of white supremacy but to control the inheritance of property. The sexual predilections of our nation's great men threatened to transfer the wealth of white male rapists to the children born of their crimes through black female bodies.

Today much has changed and much has not. The strict legal restriction of inheritable black deviance has been disrupted, but there still exists a racialized, material value of sexual relationships. The family unit is considered the basic unit for society not just because some god decreed it, but because the inheritance of accumulated privilege maintains our social order.

Thus, who we marry at the individual level may be about love, but at the group level it is also about wealth and power and privilege.

Black feminists have critiqued the material advantage that accrues to white women as a function of their elevated status as the normative cultural beauty ideal. As far as privileges go, it is certainly a complicated one, but that does not negate its utility. Being suitably marriageable privileges white women's relation to white male wealth and power.

The cultural dominance of a few acceptable brown female beauty ideals is a threat to that privilege. Cyrus acts out her faux bisexual performance for the white male gaze against a backdrop of dark, fat black female bodies and not slightly more normative cafe au lait slim bodies because the juxtaposition of her sexuality with theirs is meant to *highlight* Cyrus, not challenge her supremacy. Consider it the racialized pop culture version of a bride insisting that all of her bridesmaids be hideously clothed so as to enhance the bride's supremacy on her wedding day.

Only, rather than an ugly dress, fat black female bodies are wedded to their flesh. We cannot take it off when we desire the spotlight for ourselves or when we'd rather not be in the spotlight at all.

This political economy of specific types of black female bodies as a white amusement park was ignored by many, mostly because to critique it we have to critique ourselves.

When I moved to Atlanta I was made aware of a peculiar pastime of the city's white frat boy elite. They apparently enjoy getting drunk and visiting one of the city's many legendary black strip clubs rather than the white strip clubs. The fun part of this ritual seems to be rooted in the peculiarity of black female bodies, their athleticism, and how hard they are willing to work for less money as opposed to the more normative white strippers who expect higher wages in exchange for just looking pretty naked. There are similar racialized patterns in porn actresses' pay and, I suspect, among all manner of sex workers. The black strip clubs are a bargain good time because the value of black sexuality is discounted relative to the acceptability of black women as legitimate partners.

There is no risk of falling in love with a stripper when you're a white guy at the black strip club. Just as country music artists strip "badonkadonk" from black beauty ideals to make it palatable for their white audiences, these frat boys visit the black body wonderland as an oddity to protect the supremacy of white women as the embodiment of more and better capital.

My mentor likes to joke that interracial marriage would only be a solution to racial wealth gaps if all white men suddenly were to marry up with poor black women. It's funny because it is so ridiculous to even imagine. Sex is one thing. Marrying confers status and wealth. Slaveholders knew that. Our law reflects their knowing this. The *de rigueur* delineation of this difference may have faded, but cultural ideology remains.

Cyrus's choice of the kind of black bodies to foreground her white female sexuality was remarkable for how consistent it is with these historical patterns. . . . I believe there is something common to the bodies that are made invisible so that Cyrus might be the most visible and to our cultural denigration of bodies like mine as inferior, nonthreatening spaces where white women can play at being "dirty" without risking their sexual appeal.

I am no real threat to white women's desirability. Thus, white women have no problem cheering their husbands and boyfriends as they touch me on the dance floor. I am never seriously a contender for acceptable partner and mate for the white men who ask if their buddy can put his face in my cleavage. I am the thrill of a roller coaster with safety bars: all adrenaline but never any risk of falling to the ground.

I am not surprised that so many overlooked this particular performance of brown bodies as white amusement parks in Cyrus's performance. The whole point is that those round black female bodies are hyper-visible en masse but individually invisible to white men who were, I suspect, Cyrus's intended audience.

No, it's not Syria, but it is still worth commenting on when in the pop culture circus the white woman is the ringleader and the women who look like you are the dancing elephants.

This post originally appeared on tressiemc.com *on August 27, 2013.*

violence and masculinity threat

TRISTAN BRIDGES AND C.J. PASCOE

n April 2014, in Milford, Connecticut, Chris Plaskon asked Maren Sanchez to attend prom with him at the end of the year at Jonathan Law High School. They'd known each other since sixth grade. Maren said no. Witnesses told authorities she declined and told Chris she would be attending the dance with her boyfriend. Chris threw his hands around Maren's throat, pushed her down a set of stairs, and cut and stabbed her with a kitchen knife he'd brought to school. It was April 25, 2014. Maren got to school just a bit after 7:00 that day, and before 8:00 she was dead.

This tragic, almost unfathomable violence reminds us of so many stories of adolescent male violence over the past couple decades. Jackson Katz discusses a seeming epidemic of violence among young white men in his new film *Tough Guise 2*. In analyzing the tragedies of school shootings, Katz tells us that we need to think about them as contemporary forms of masculinity. When young men have their masculinity sullied, threatened, or denied, they respond by reclaiming masculinity through a highly recognizable masculine practice: violence. It's easy to paint the young men who perpetuate these crimes as psychologically disturbed, as—importantly—unlike the rest of us. But stories like Chris Plaskon's follow what has become a predictable pattern.

Sociologists address this as a form of "social identity threat." The general idea is that when you threaten someone's social identity and that person cares, they respond by over-demonstrating qualities that illustrate their membership in that identity. In *Theorizing Masculinities*, Michael Kimmel writes about a classic example:

> I have a standing bet with a friend that I can walk onto any playground in America where 6-year-old boys are happily playing and by asking one question, I can provoke a fight. That question is simple: "Who's a sissy around here?"

While you might think Kimmel's offering easy money here, he's making a larger point. Kimmel is inviting someone's masculinity to be threatened and assuming that this will require someone to demonstrate their masculinity in dramatic fashion. Sociologists have a name for this phenomenon: *masculinity threat*. New research relying on experimental designs suggests there's a lot more to these claims than first meets the eye.

For instance, Christin Munsch and Robb Willer conducted an experiment, reported in the journal *Violence Against Women*, to see whether gender identity threats might affect perceptions of sexual coercion. College-aged respondents took a survey assessing how "masculine" or "feminine" they were. They received feedback quickly, but the feedback wasn't honest: students were randomly assigned to receive scores that either confirmed or challenged their gender identity. This is where the *real* study began. Students were told to next fill out a "campus climate" survey regarding their opinions about different cases that had been brought before a campus disciplinary review board. One of the cases dealt with sexual coercion. Their study clearly showed that when college-aged men's masculinity was threatened, they were much more likely to espouse attitudes supportive of sexual assault or coercion. In a nutshell, men who might feel they have to demonstrate their masculinity are much more likely to blame the victim (a woman) in the scenario.

In an *American Journal of Sociology* article, Robb Willer, Bridget Conlon, Christabel Rogalin, and Michael Wojnowicz test what they refer to as the "masculine overcompensation thesis." The research illustrates the validity of Kimmel's playground bet and proves that the effects are farther reaching than we may have expected. . . . Threatened men were more supportive of the Iraq War, expressed more sexual prejudice toward homosexuals, and were even more likely to say they wanted to buy an SUV! These men were also much more likely to believe in the inherent superiority of males. Perhaps interestingly, for sociologists, men with the highest testosterone levels in this study showed the strongest effects.

Catherine Taylor's recent research, reported in *Social Science & Medicine*, builds on their interesting finding about hormones by considering men's physiological responses to masculinity threats. Taylor brought men and women into a lab and had them work in small groups to solve small problems together. Taylor was interested in the physiological responses of having some social influence (or lacking it) and varied the sex composition of the groups. Men were much more likely to exhibit anxiety and stress if they failed to achieve high social status in a group with other men but not with women. Taylor's work is a powerful demonstration of how gender ideologies not only affect our social experiences and opportunities; they quite literally get inside of us. Taylor's research also suggests that the men with higher levels of testosterone in the previous study might actually be illustrating the way in which these responses to masculinity threats have become a permanent part of their physiology. In other words, testosterone isn't so much the cause of violence as it is produced by gender inequality.

This is an important body of research that helps us think about the relationship between masculinity and violence. When we hear about cases in the news like the savage murder of Maren Sanchez, the easy way of dealing with this is to look for all of the signs that Chris Plaskon is not "one of us." But Katz and Kimmel suggest that we ought to think about these men not as failing at masculinity but as "over-conforming," and research supports those claims.

For a long time, feminist scholars and activists talked about violence among boys and men as "learned behavior." This research shows how well most men have learned this lesson. In *Tough Guise 2*, Katz reiterates this issue but follows by reminding us that violence is also a *"taught* behavior." And these lessons are not just taught by individuals; they're a part of all manner of social institutions. They structure the ways we learn to think about, recognize, and enact masculinity in our daily lives. We simply can't think about violence apart from gender.

This article originally appeared on Girl w/ Pen! *on May 7, 2014.*

gender and biased perceptions: scientists rate job applicants

GWEN SHARP

A study titled "Science Faculty's Subtle Gender Biases Favor Male Students" shows compelling evidence for unconscious gender bias among faculty, specifically in some natural and biological science fields. The researchers asked a national sample of 127 biology, physics, and chemistry professors to evaluate the application materials of an undergrad science student who applied for a lab manager position, a job they saw as a gateway to other opportunities. Everyone was given the same materials, but half the applicants were given the first name Jennifer and half John. The participants were told the student would be given feedback based on their evaluations.

The results are sobering. There was a significant difference in the average competence, hireability, and mentoring

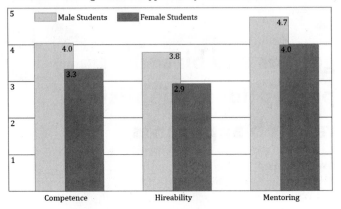

Scientists' Ranking of Student Applicants by Students' Gender

Source: Adapted from Moss-Racusin et al. 2012
Notes: Scale ranges from 1-7; scores are rounded
Graphic created for TheSocietyPages.org by Suzy McElrath

ratings by gender. Professors who thought they were evaluating a female applicant saw a less qualified candidate.

So not only was there a gap in perceived competence and fit for the position, but professors were less willing to engage in the type of mentoring that can help students gain both skills and confidence in their abilities—which can be especially important for underrepresented groups.

And despite what you might expect, female professors were just as likely to do this as male professors were. Professors' age, tenure status, and discipline didn't make a difference either.

The professors were also asked to recommend a starting salary. The average suggested beginning salary for the male candidate was $30,238, while for the female student it was $26,507.

The authors point out that these findings are especially noteworthy because this sample was made up of scientists who are active in their fields, regularly working with students.

Interestingly, when asked how much they *liked* the candidate, those evaluating the female student gave a higher score than those assigned the male student. But this didn't translate into seeing the female candidate as competent. The study authors argue that this is strong evidence for subtle gender bias. The professors didn't express dislike or hostility toward a female candidate. In fact, they tended to actively like her. But as the researchers explained,

Despite expressing warmth toward emerging female scientists, faculty members of both genders appear to be affected by enduring cultural stereotypes about women's lack of

Recommended Starting Salary by Applicant's Gender

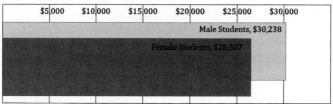

Source: Adapted from Moss-Racusin et al. 2012
Notes: Salary reported in US dollars
Graphic created for TheSocietyPages.org by Suzy McElrath

science competence that translate into biases in student evaluation and mentoring. (p. 4)

This study implies that women in the natural and biological sciences (and surely other fields) still face prejudices that can impact the opportunities they are given to work closely with professors to gain important experiences and skills, as well as limit their access to jobs and affect their pay. These factors can snowball over time, creating larger and larger gaps in career achievements and income as men capitalize on opportunities while women find it impossible to catch up.

This article originally appeared on Sociological Images *on September 26, 2012.*

my two cents on feminism and miley cyrus

LISA WADE

Oddly, three high-profile female musicians find themselves in a public debate about what it means to be a feminist. We can thank Miley Cyrus for the occasion. After claiming that the video for her song "Wrecking Ball" was inspired by Sinead O'Connor's video for her cover of "Nothing Compares 2 U," O'Connor wrote an open letter to the performer. She argued that the music industry would inevitably exploit Cyrus's body and leave her a shell of a human being. Amanda Palmer, another strong-minded female musician, responded to O'Connor. She countered with the idea that all efforts to control women's choices, no matter how benevolent, were anti-feminist.

I think they're both right, but only half right. Both letters are kind, compelling, and smart, but neither capture the deep contradictions that Cyrus—indeed all women in the United States—face every day.

O'Connor warns that the music industry is patriarchal and capitalist.... The whole point is to exploit her. Meanwhile, her exploitation will be distinctly gendered, because sexism is part of the very fabric of the industry. O'Connor writes:

> The music business doesn't give a shit about you, or any of us. They will prostitute you for all you are worth ... and when you end up in rehab as a result of being prostituted, "they" will be sunning themselves on their yachts in Antigua, which they bought by selling your body.

Whether Cyrus ends up in rehab remains to be seen, but O'Connor is, of course, right about the music industry. This is not something that requires argumentation but is simply true in a patriarchal, capitalist society. For-profit industries are *for profit*. You may think that's good or bad, but it is, by definition, about finding ways to extract money from goods and services, selling a product for more than you paid for it. And media companies of all kinds are dominated at almost all levels by (rich, white) men. These are the facts.

Palmer, in turn, claims that O'Connor is contributing to an oppressive environment for women. All women's choices, Palmer argues, should be considered fair game:

I want to live in a world where WE as women determine what we wear and look like and play the game as our fancy leads us, army pants one minute and killer gown the next, where WE decide whether or not we're going to play games with the male gaze.

In Palmer's utopia, no one gets to decide what's best for women. The whole point is to have all options on the table, without censure, so women can pick and choose and change their minds as they so desire.

This is intuitively pleasing and seems to mesh pretty well with a decent definition of "freedom." And women do have more choices—many, many more choices—than recent generations of women. They are now free to vote in elections, wear pants, smoke in public, have their own bank accounts, play sports, go into men's occupations and, yes, be unabashedly sexual. Hell, they can even run for president. And they get to still do all the feminine stuff too!

So both are making a feminist argument. What, then, is the source of the disagreement? O'Connor and Palmer are using different levels of analysis. Palmer's is straightforwardly *individualistic*: each individual woman should be able to choose what she wants to do. O'Connor's is strongly *institutional*: we are all operating within a system—the music industry, in this case, or even "society"—and that system is powerfully deterministic.

The truth is that both are right and, because of that, neither sees the whole picture. On the one hand, women *are* making individual choices. They are not complete dupes of the system. They are architects of their own lives. On the other hand, those individual choices *are* being made within a system. The system sets up the pros and cons, the rewards and punishments, the paths to success and the pitfalls that lead to failure. No amount of wishing it were different will make it so. No individual choices change that reality.

So, Cyrus may indeed be "in charge of her own show," as Palmer puts it. She may have chosen to be a "raging, naked, twerking sexpot" all of her own volition. But why? Because that's what the system rewards. That's not freedom; that's a strategy.

In sociological terms, we call this a patriarchal bargain. Both men and women make them, and they come in many different forms. Generally, however, they involve a choice to manipulate the system to one's best advantage without challenging the system itself. This may maximize the benefits that accrue to any individual woman, but it harms women as a whole. Cyrus's particular bargain—accepting the sexual objectification of women in exchange for money, fame, and power—is a common one. We all make patriarchal bargains, large and small. Housewives do when they support husbands' careers on the agreement that they share the dividends. Many high-achieving women do when they go into masculinized occupations to reap the benefits but don't challenge the idea that occupations associated with men are of greater value. None of us has the moral high ground here.

So, is Miley Cyrus a pawn of industry patriarchs? No. Can her choices be fairly described as good for women? No.

That's how power works. It makes it so that essentially all choices can be absorbed into and mobilized on behalf of the system. Fighting the system on behalf of the disadvantaged—in this case, women—requires individual sacrifices that are extraordinarily costly (in Cyrus's case, perhaps being replaced by another artist who is willing to capitulate to patriarchy with more gusto). Accepting the rules of the system translates into individual gain but doesn't exactly make the world a better place. . . .

If the way out of this conundrum were easy, we'd have fixed it already. But one thing's for sure: it's going to take *collective* sacrifice to bring about a world in which women's humanity is so taken for granted that no individual woman's choices can undermine it. To get there, we're going to need to acknowledge the power of the system, recognize each other as conscious actors, and have empathy for the difficult choices we all make as we try to navigate a difficult world.

This article originally appeared on Sociological Images *on October 12, 2013.*

part 4: institutions

S ociologists use the word *institution* to refer to combinations of policies and practices ingrained in daily life that aim to fulfill collective needs. The physical network of roads and highways, for example, together with sources of funding, bureaucratic processes, and individuals on the ground enforcing laws, laying asphalt, maintaining streetlights, and more, make up the institution of transportation. Since we can't all lay our own roads or keep ourselves safe in the absence of order, we've built an entire edifice to take care of this need for all of us.

There are many more examples. Health care, homeland defense, and the news industry are some. Each is characterized by persistent patterns of social interaction that enable and constrain our daily lives. Stability in institutions occurs both because of habit and formal laws and policies that guide our behavior. We file our taxes, for example, not out of habit, but because there are laws requiring that we do so and penalties if we do not. That's an example of a way that institutions can impose formal requirements. Others secure our compliance more through habit, like the institutionalized practice of celebrating national holidays. There are no laws or punishments, but we, alongside millions of our fellow citizens, often participate in the ritual nonetheless.

Institutions generally organize so much of life that opting out is essentially impossible. You want to fly a commercial airline? You have to contend with Homeland Security. You want to become a doctor? You have to pass through higher education. You want to own a house? You have to deal with the financial industry.

Institutions are also gendered, meaning that the logic of the gender binary often informs their organization. Fashion is a great example. When we enter a department store—ones like Macy's, Dillard's, and JC Penney—space is divided up by gender. There is no law that requires clothing manufacturers to make *women's* and *men's clothes*, as opposed to *clothes*. Nor do men's and women's bodies come in a binary that requires them to do so. Most of us have two arms, two legs, and a torso; some of us are fat and some skinny, some tall and some short. Some of us have boobs and others don't, but none of this, sometimes to our chagrin, aligns perfectly with what genitals we have.

Still, designers design and manufacturers produce essentially zero items of just plain clothing; all items are either made for women or made for men. Department stores, in response, organize their clothing selection into men's and women's sections. Designers, then, make more clothes that will fit into the organization of the department store. Most of the time people go there and buy clothes from the "right" section out of habit or fear. Because those clothes are designed to make our bodies conform to gendered expectations, we do gender by default. And so the circle is closed.

In the rest of this section, we take a closer look at other gendered institutions—sport, health, education, work, reproduction, and politics—to try to understand how they shape our lives and identities.

—LISA WADE

woman enough to win?

CHERYL COOKY AND SHARI L. DWORKIN

The 2012 Summer Olympic Games in London were the first in which female athletes were represented in all events and the first in which female athletes from Saudi Arabia participated. Despite these improvements, the Olympics represent a paradox that produces two different outcomes with respect to women's sport: on the one hand, female athletes and women's sport, especially here in the United States, receive more (and more respectful) media coverage during Olympic years. As *New York Times* journalist Frank Bruni wrote, the Olympics are where "girl power gets its sweaty, sinewy due." Indeed, in these weeks, women experience a degree of parity with their male counterparts, serving as proud representatives of the nation-state.

However, in some ways, it's this sense of nationalism that has contributed to the establishment of sex-testing policies in women's sports. By raising the visibility of female athletes and women's sport, national pride and athletic equity in the Olympics have increased surveillance of female athletes, who have found themselves subject to sex testing for eligibility. It's all well and good for women to gain the spotlight, the argument seemed to go, but they must be protected from their international rivals who might hold a hidden advantage: they might be technically (in any number of difficult-to-spot ways) male.

Thus, the significance of South African star Caster Semenya, running for Olympic gold in the 800-meter finals in London's 2012 Games.

In post-apartheid South Africa, sport has played a significant role in nation-building and in helping to stabilize the country during a time of transitional democracy. Black women helped bring together various national identities both within sport and in the wider society in South Africa. As both a black woman and an athlete on the international stage, then, Caster Semenya has been an important national icon—she was even the first black South African woman to win a gold medal at an IAAF World Championship. Given her upbringing in an impoverished rural town with high unemployment and her international success in sport, Semenya served in many ways as a powerful embodiment of the ascendency of the "new" South Africa. Thus, when she was accused of not being a "real" woman at the 2009 IAAF World

Championships, it caused such a controversy even South Africa's president spoke out on her behalf, asserting and solidifying both her gender identity and her position as a representative of the nation-state. Fans, politicians, and South Africans of all stripes claimed Semenya as their "Golden Girl," "Our First Lady of Sport."

As intriguing as her story is on its own terms, Semenya's is just one of the most recent and famous chapters in a much larger, longer-running controversy surrounding sex testing in international Olympic sport.

looking back

In the early twentieth century, women's participation in sport competitions dramatically increased, as did the quality of their performances. During the Cold War, countries used sport to justify and legitimize the economic, political, and social organization of capitalist and communist societies, and women's sport participation found itself at the center of an ideological war. Images of feminine athletes from the United States were juxtaposed with those of their "manly" competitors from the Soviet Bloc. For the first time, questions were raised regarding the sex of the participants in women's competitions. Capitalist countries suspected communist countries of not fielding "real" women (an assertion based solely on appearance) ... a violation of the purity, fairness, and sanctity of sport. These concerns and the high political stakes of international competition at the time eventually led to the implementation of mandatory sex-testing policies. ...

The International Olympic Committee (IOC) implemented mandatory sex testing in 1968, and the policy continued until the 2000 Olympic Games. The first sex tests (performed prior to mandatory testing) involved an often humiliating physical and visual inspection of the genitals. Advances in technology, specifically the Barr body (chromosome) test and later the polymerase chain reaction (PCR) test of the SRY gene, eliminated reliance on just a visual inspection, but biomedical experts have noted the weakness of these tests to identify or determine sex/gender. At a basic level, the tests are known for false positives. For example, in the 1996 Summer Olympics in Atlanta, eight of over 3,000 female athletes tested "positive" (that is, suspect, gender-wise) using the PCR test. Yet, all eight athletes were allowed to compete, as further medical testing determined that the athletes did not hold an "unfair advantage." Over time, biomedical scientists came to believe sex testing of *any* type was insufficient for determining "real" sex, because sex itself is comprised of multiple components, including genes, chromosomes, hormones, and genitalia. ...

Despite ongoing concerns of medical professionals, the prevalence of false positives and the use of tests that do not conclusively determine sex, and the challenge of developing a sound procedure to determine an athlete's sex (assuming that's possible or desirable), the IOC and other sport-governing bodies continue with policies that allow for the testing of athletes or the monitoring of participants in women's competitions. One aspect of the policy that *has* changed is that sex tests are no longer mandatory for female athletes (as of the 2000 Olympics). Another change is that the IOC no longer claims to test or verify the sex of the athlete. Instead, according to the most recent IOC policy, the concern resides in the *androgen* levels of female athletes.

It should be noted here that athletes in male events have never had to undergo any gender verification or sex test. The IOC assumes that no woman could possibly outperform a man, so there's no concern a female athlete might masquerade as (and compete at an Olympic level against) a male. Indeed, the IOC's "Regulations on Female Hyperandrogenism," released in June 2012, states that the "performances of male and female athletes may differ mainly due to the fact that men produce significantly more androgenic hormones than women and, therefore, are under stronger influence of such hormones." Hence, the 2012 astonishment and outcry when 16-year-old female Chinese swimmer Ye Shiwen clocked a lap time faster than that of U.S. champion Ryan Lochte in Olympic competition. However, since only athletes entering women's competitive events are tested or monitored, it seems the policies rest on an assumption of natural, categorical male superiority.

rationalizing inequity

Given the apparent belief in the natural physical superiority of male athletes, a main rationale used by sports organizational bodies regarding the need for sex testing or monitoring of female athletes is the need to ensure a level playing field by policing any "unfair advantages" athletes in women's competitions may have. Historically, the rationale was more explicit: it was meant to prevent men from disguising themselves as women and, well, beating them. But where there's a policy, usually there's a precedent.

The most frequently—and only—cited case of such sporting shenanigans occurred in the 1936 Berlin Olympics. Hermann (Dora) Ratjen, a man, was forced by German officials to compete in the women's high jump event disguised as a woman. Despite his "advantage," Ratjen placed only fourth— all three medal winners were female.... Since then, with more intricate testing, there have been several high-profile examples of female athletes who "failed" a sex test and were determined to not be "real" females. Often they experienced no competitive advantage, yet medals were revoked and the athletes were banned from competition.

In another odd aspect of modern sex testing, the IOC has enacted its sex-determination policies but seems to tolerate a myriad of other advantages that could be deemed unfair. For example, several basketball players have a condition called acromegaly, which is responsible for excessive tallness. Likewise, a number of female volleyball players have been found to have Marfan's syndrome, a disorder that contributes to unusual height. For his part, endurance skier Eero Mantyranta has an inherited genetic mutation that causes high hemoglobin and increased oxygen capacity—a clear advantage in his sport.

And while the IOC is concerned with the androgen levels of female athletes, the same concern does not extend to men. Other than testing for exogenous levels of testosterone (which would indicate doping or steroid use), the IOC and other international governing bodies are not concerned with the *endogenic* testosterone levels of male athletes. The IOC's 2012 policy claims that "androgenic hormones have performance-enhancing effects, particularly on strength, power and speed, which may provide a competitive advantage in sports" (a contested claim as sport performance is the result of an endless intersection of factors that include not only physiology but also training, diet, facilities, equipment, and so on). So, if we accept the IOC's logic, it is curious why the governing body might not be concerned that at least some males are "too male" to compete.

how inequity breeds inequity

Sport has played an important cultural role regarding the ostensible "proof" of the "naturalness" of gender difference. Indeed, cultural assumptions about the differences between men and women are so much a part of athletic competition at all levels that we almost never even recognize them at all. But it is male dominance more than gender difference that is also most often at stake in sport.

The belief in the categorical superiority of men actually helped shape the development of sport in the United States in the 1800s. . . . Sport historians note that the formation of sport (and other male-only institutions such as the Boy Scouts and the YMCA) helped assuage fears of the perceived feminization of boys and men. . . . In turn, girls and women were mostly denied access, due to fears that sport would "masculinize" them and, of course, because they were "physically inferior" anyway. (It is worth recalling that there was no women's Olympic marathon until 1984; until then, medical experts deemed that women were vulnerable to reproductive problems if they were to complete a 26.2-mile course.)

This sort of history explains why women's entrance into the coveted fields of male-dominated sport has been so contested. Even as women's participation has increased at all competitive levels, it continues to challenge what our society believes women are capable of, as well as their appropriate societal roles. It also reaffirms cultural beliefs about the "natural," physical inferiority of women. Because of this, sport sociologist Michael Messner has called female athletes "contested terrain," and other scholars have drawn attention to the ways in which female athletes must negotiate a complex array of societal expectations of femininity within sport's values, norms, and behaviors (all of which have historically been associated with masculinity).

Because sport has been lauded as a way to make boys into men, when women participate—especially when they excel—there is a secondary problem. They are hypersexualized and hyper-feminized, accused of being lesbians, or presumed to really be men. Checking to verify that female athletes are in fact "real" women, while assuming that all male athletes in sport are "real" men, comes out of and reinforces the belief that "real" women cannot possibly be outstanding athletes. A belief that gender disparities have merit upholds, among other inequities in sport, sex-testing policies.

leveling the field

Elsewhere we have argued that if sports governing bodies insist on monitoring athletes' gender, the policy should be applied equally and consistently. Male athletes with levels of testosterone or androgens that exceed the "normal male range" should also be prevented from participating as male athletes in men's competitions. Given the IOC's logic, this would ensure a level playing field in men's events. Interestingly, though, the IOC has not released a policy regarding what constitutes a "normal" range of male testosterone. But, of course, this argument is a rhetorical device: testosterone is only an advantage to the extent that the body and muscles can respond to it. For example, female athletes with androgen insensitivity disorder (a condition that would have resulted in a "failed" sex test under prior sex-testing policies) are actually at a disadvantage because their bodies cannot respond to circulating androgens. In other words, androgen or testosterone levels alone do not indicate an "unfair advantage" in sport any more than a height above six feet is an "unfair advantage" for a volleyball or basketball player.

Further, sport scientists note that excellence in sport is a complex combination of biology, talent, diet, training, access to opportunity, equipment, facilities, and a myriad of other factors that cannot be controlled or monitored. As a result, some have posed the important and frustrating question: Can the IOC maintain a level playing field? Considering biology alone, many athletes might be unable to compete; most, if not all, elite athletes are genetic outliers. As geneticist Eric Vilain observed, "If athletes were just average, sports would lack the allure and capital they currently enjoy."

One way to address discriminatory sex-testing policies is to acknowledge how much sporting competition relies upon very traditional gender binaries and dualisms, distinctions that obligate men and women to compete separately (not to mention that impose a dualistic categorization scheme that may not always fully capture the complexity and variation among individual human beings). Another perhaps even more important intervention is to realize that sport is not now and has never been a "level playing field." This admission may prove beneficial, and not just for the athletes who are subject to sex-, gender-, and hormone-monitoring policies. The myth of sport as a level playing field reproduces other forms of inequalities, including racism, economic inequality, able-ism, and others. Contemporary sport institutions and organizations are rife with inequalities that are accepted as part of the game (for example, better economic resources confer better access to training facilities, equipment, and coaches—all of which enhance sport performance).

Thus, rather than testing athletes to ensure no one has an "unfair advantage" in women's competitions, we could accept that sport is never a level playing field, which would, in turn, eliminate any need to test athletes, male or female, in the first place.

Scientific experts acknowledge that the IOC and other sports-governing bodies that implement sex testing are making a "reasoned choice among many imperfect options." We believe that alone offers a compelling rationale to eliminate sex testing of female athletes.

This article originally appeared as a peer-reviewed white paper on The Society Pages *on August 10, 2012.*

19

our hearts, our selves, our research agenda

TINA PITTMAN WAGERS

am new to this role as a heart patient. My heart attack was five weeks ago, and I am getting the feeling that I have just begun down the confusing maze of angiograms, CT scans, EKGs, medications, heart-rate monitors, cardiac rehab classes, and blood tests. Indeed, even the phrase "my cardiologist" is one I never thought would pass my lips. Here's why: I am 53 (we'll discuss the significance of this age in a moment). I am fit, active, slim, haven't eaten red meat for about 20 years and am a big fan of kale, salmon, and quinoa, much to the chagrin of my two teenage sons. I live near the foothills in Boulder, Colorado, where I hike almost every day. I had completed a sprint triathlon two weeks before my heart attack. . . .

My heart attack happened while I was swimming across a lake in Cascade, Idaho. I was about a quarter mile into the swim when I found that I couldn't breathe, and was grabbed by an oddly cold and simultaneously searing band of pain about three inches wide across my sternum. My husband, Ken, was on a paddleboard nearby and helped pull me out of the water, and started paddling me back, stopping to allow me to vomit on the way back to shore. . . . Suffice to say that I am grateful for Ken's strength and balance in innumerable ways. An hour later, I was at a clinic in McCall, Idaho, where an astute ER doc was measuring my heart rate (very low) and heart attack–indicative enzyme called troponin (rising), so I won an ambulance ride to St. Luke's Hospital in Boise, Idaho. I received excellent care there, queued up for an angiogram the next morning, and was diagnosed with SCAD: a spontaneous coronary artery dissection (fortunately, a relatively mild one). Twenty percent of SCADs are fatal.

I have none of the typical risk factors for heart disease, like high blood pressure, diabetes, or high cholesterol. I do have one of the main risk factors for this kind of heart attack, though: *I am a woman.* The average SCAD patient is 42, female, and is without other typical risk factors for heart attacks. The current thinking about SCADs is that they are not as rare as originally thought but are underdiagnosed because they happen in women who don't look like typical heart patients.

Another related factor: *I am menopausal.* The majority of SCAD patients are postpartum, close to their menstrual cycle, or menopausal—all times in women's lives during which we experience significant fluctuations of sex hormones. Up until five days before my heart attack, I had been on low doses of hormone replacement therapy (HRT) in an effort to vanquish the hot flashes, sleep disruption, and cognitive fogginess I was experiencing. I suppose HRT might have also represented an attempt to hang on to youth, in a youth- and sexuality-obsessed culture in which the transition to menopause often means a dysregulated and sweaty march into irrelevance.

Since I had my heart attack, I've spent a lot of time (and money, but that's another column) interacting with professionals in the cardiology world, trying to figure out what happened to me and how I can avoid having another SCAD (the rate of recurrence in my population is about 20–50%). Almost all of them are *baffled* about what to do with me. I am atypical, as they inevitably explain, but the medications, the treatments, the rehab programs that they have to offer are designed for typical patients. So there is a lot of "voodoo vs. science," as one cardiologist explained, because science doesn't have the answers to my questions. . . .

Why do we know so little about women and heart attacks, why they happen, what the symptoms are, and what we can do about hormonal factors that contribute? A big part of the problem is that, until the National Institutes of Health (NIH) Revitalization Act in 1993, researchers largely excluded female humans from their studies. It was only in 2014 that the NIH decided to use a balance of male and female cells and animals in their research. Up until then, 90% of the animal research was conducted on males. Animal research, which is often a precursor to clinical trials in humans, has been missing out on vast pieces of investigation related to the female body. I am living (fortunately) proof of the fact that the delays in including females in research have translated into significant gaps in clinically relevant knowledge related to women's health. Well-meaning physicians and practitioners only have the "typical" approaches to try with their "atypical" patients. Why this appalling delay to include female subjects? Because female rodents as well as humans experience menstruation and menopause, which are frequently considered dysregulating nuisances to many scientists. As a consequence, we have an enormous amount of catching up to do in order to understand what factors affect female bodies and health problems in different ways than those of our male peers.

The actress Emma Watson gave a great talk at the UN about feminism meaning equal access to resources. One of the most important resources we have is scientific knowledge that can be applied to responsible, effective, and efficient clinical care. Let's hope that women can start to be understood as typical research subjects and patients, not as inconvenient, fluctuating, atypical anomalies.

This article originally appeared on Girl w/ Pen! *on September 29, 2014.*

is the "mrs." degree dead?

LAURA T. HAMILTON

n 1998 I was a first-year student at DePauw University, a
small liberal arts college in Indiana. A floor-mate of mine,
with whom I hung out occasionally, told me over lunch that
she was at college primarily to find a "good husband." I nearly
choked on my sandwich.... Surely [the "Mrs." degree] had
gone the way of the home economics major and women's
dormitory curfews.

Years later, I—along with my co-director, Elizabeth A.
Armstrong—would embark on a five-year ethnographic and
longitudinal study of a dormitory floor of women at a public
flagship in the Midwest. As part of my dissertation, I also
interviewed the women's parents. [It] brought me back to
my first year of college. A subset of parents wanted their
daughters to be "cookie-baking moms"—not successful law-
yers, doctors, or businesswomen. They espoused *gender
complementarity*—a cultural model of how women should

achieve economic security that relies on a co-constructed pairing of traditional femininity and masculinity. That is, men were to be economic providers and women supportive homemakers.

This was a *revised* Mrs. degree, in the sense that marriage during college, or even right after, was not desirable. College women were to build the traits and social networks that would hopefully land them a successful husband *eventually*, but it was assumed best to wait until men had proven themselves in the labor market before entering a marriage.

This was not the only cultural model to which women on the floor were exposed. In fact, those coming in primed for complementarity were in the minority. However, as I show in my 2014 *Gender & Society* article "The Revised MRS: Gender Complementarity at College," far more women *left* college leaning toward gender complementarity. Something was happening on the college campus—where women were, ironically, outachieving men—that shifted them toward performing an affluent, white, heterosexual femininity, marked by an emphasis on appearance, accommodation to men, and a bubbly personality.

I argue that gender complementarity is not just a characteristic of individual women but is actually encouraged by the institutional and interactional features of the typical four-year public state school. Midwest U, like other schools of its kind, builds a social and academic infrastructure well suited to high-paying, out-of-state students interested in partying. The predominately white Greek system—a historically gender-, class-, and racially segregated institution—enjoys prominence on campus. An array of "easy" majors, geared toward characteristics developed outside of the classroom, allows women to leverage personality, looks, and social skills in the academic sphere. These supports make it possible for peer cultures in which gender complementarity is paramount to thrive. Women who want to belong and make friends find it hard—if not impossible—to avoid the influence of the dominant social scene on campus, located in fraternities and Greek-oriented bars.

This structure of campus life is not incidental. In recent years, cuts to state and federal support for higher education have led mid-tier public institutions like Midwest U to cater to the socially oriented and out-of-state students who arrive with gender complementarity interests. These class-based processes have implications for the type of social and academic climate that all students find upon arriving at Midwest University.

The problem is, however, that most women need to accrue the skills and credentials that translate into a solid career. An institution supporting gender complementarity does them a serious disservice—potentially contributing to gendered differences in pay after college. The situation is particularly problematic for students not from the richest of families: Affluent women espousing complementarity form the type of networks that give them reasonable hope of rescue by a high-credentialed spouse, and heavy parental support means that they can afford to be in big cities where they mix and mingle with the "right" men. Women from less affluent backgrounds lack these resources and are often reliant on their own human capital to make it after college.

The gradual shift from higher education as a public good (funded heavily by the state) to a private commodity (for sale to the highest bidder) has significantly stalled not only progress toward class equality but certain forms of gender equality as well. Change is going to require unlinking the solvency of organizations like Midwest U from the interests of those who can afford, and thus demand, an exclusionary and highly gendered social experience.

This article originally appeared on the Gender & Society *blog on April 2, 2014.*

gender and the sinking floor in the u.s. labor market

ERIN HATTON

n her *New York Times* article "How Can We Help Men? By Helping Women," historian Stephanie Coontz argues that workplace policies construed as helping women workers are, in fact, crucial for *all* workers. Such policies include increasing the minimum wage to a "livable wage," making good child care available and affordable, extending unemployment benefits to part-time and temporary workers, and strengthening the social safety net to better support families in poverty. These are . . . only misconstrued as "women's issues" because of an outdated paradigm of male breadwinning and female domesticity. The reality today, of course, is that both men and women work, and both are struggling to support themselves and their families. "The most urgent issue facing working Americans today is not the glass ceiling," Coontz writes. "It is the sinking floor."

I agree. True, the "glass ceiling" is a major obstacle for many women workers, and a "glass escalator" unfairly lifts too many men to the top of the pay and promotion scale even in women-dominated jobs. But at this historical moment, the most *urgent* issue for men and women workers (and their children) is the sinking floor.

Yet I have reservations about packaging the solutions to this problem as "putting women first." As Coontz persuasively demonstrates, these policies are not for women alone. It is not putting *women* first to increase the minimum wage, expand the availability of child care, extend unemployment benefits to part-time workers, and strengthen the social safety net. Such policies put *people* first—women, men, and children—and preserving their construction as women's issues risks unintentionally reifying the longstanding employer fiction that women are a special category of workers . . . that needs protection (e.g., bans on heavy lifting and long hours), requires monitoring and restriction (e.g., marriage and pregnancy bans), whose skills are innate rather than earned, and does not require a "breadwinning" wage. But while women have faced—and continue to face—unique challenges and obstacles in the workforce, they are not a distinct category of worker. And though casting them as such has long been a successful strategy to secure low-wage labor, doing so has far-reaching negative consequences.

Whenever employers successfully carve out one category of worker as *different from* "real" workers, not only is that category of worker at greater risk of exploitation, so are *all* workers.

In my book *The Temp Economy*, I examine how the fledgling temp industry strategically deployed gender, racial, and class ideologies to sell temp work in the 1950s and '60s. This strategy, I argue, did much more than establish a new sector of low-wage, dead-end, pink-collar work: It helped undermine (traditionally male) "breadwinning" employment.

In the years after World War II, the early leaders of the new temporary help industry successfully gained entrée into the labor market by constructing temp work as white middle-class "women's work." Temp work, the founders of Manpower, Kelly Girl, and other agencies proclaimed, was for white middle-class housewives who had nothing better to do. They were not "real" workers; they were simply dabbling in temp work in their spare time to buy a few luxuries. The title of a 1956 article in *Good Housekeeping*, "Extra Money for Extra Work for Extra Women," perfectly summarized the temp industry's marketing strategy.

In truth, however, most women in the 1950s and '60s did not temp for "extra" money; rather, they temped to support their families. Moreover, women weren't the only ones working in temp jobs. By the early 1960s the two largest temp agencies employed plenty of men: Fully 40% of Manpower's workers were men, and Kelly Girl Services had launched "Labor Aides" and other company branches to employ male industrial temps.

Nonetheless, describing temp work—and temp workers—as "extra" was pervasive in industry marketing campaigns. This strategy was ingenious because, in the American cultural imagination, *it made sense*: White middle-class housewives weren't seen as "real" workers. It was assumed that they didn't have to work, and their only real job—as we saw it—was raising their children and taking care of their husbands and home. . . . Temp agency work gained both cultural and legal legitimacy.

This legitimacy enabled the temp industry to push far beyond the pink-collar sector, in both rhetoric and reality. In the 1970s the temp industry stopped marketing "extra women" to do "extra work." Instead, industry leaders urged employers to replace all permanent employees—men and women, secretaries and CEOs—with temps. They argued that permanent employees were "costly burdens," "expensive headaches." . . . By providing employers with a steady stream of low-cost, no-liability temps, the temporary help industry gave employers the tools to put this rhetoric into action. Temporary employment skyrocketed in the 1970s and continued apace in the 1980s and '90s. Today temp work—along with many other varieties of low-wage, insecure, unstable employment—is widespread: as much as 90% of employers report using temps and temp agencies every year; nearly three million people work as "temps" in the United States every day. The temp industry has added more jobs than any other sector since the end of the most recent recession. . . .

This history suggests that designating one category of worker—first, white middle-class housewives and, later, all temps—as different from (white male) "regular" workers effectively converted those workers into an inexpensive army of reserve labor and thus contributed to a broad degradation of employment standards.

Yet women are not the only target of such divides. Today there are other categories of workers who are culturally (and often legally) constructed as different from "regular" workers, including prisoners who work while incarcerated, immigrant "guestworkers," and even interns. We must watch out for such categorizations and, in challenging those workers' exploitation, we must be careful not to rely too heavily on the socially constructed divides that made it possible. Thus, instead of packaging the solutions to the sinking wage floor as "helping women," it might be better to rethink (and complicate) the implicit binary between "men's" and "women's issues," and seek to understand in whose interests the lines between them have been drawn.

This article originally appeared on the Gender & Society *blog on March 10, 2014.*

putting hobby lobby in context: the erratic career of birth control in the united states

CAROLE JOFFE

I n the 1965 *Griswold v. Connecticut* case, the Supreme Court declared birth control legal for married persons, and shortly afterward, in another case, for single people. In a famous study published in 2002, "The Power of the Pill," two Harvard economists reported on the dramatic rise in women's entrance into the professions and attributed this development to the availability of oral contraception beginning in the 1960s. And several years ago, the CDC reported that 99% of U.S. women who have ever had sexual intercourse had used contraception at some point. So the controversial *Hobby Lobby* case no doubt appears somewhat surreal to many Americans who understandably have assumed that contraception—unlike abortion—is a settled, noncontentious issue in the United States.

To be sure, some conservatives, fearful of a female voter backlash in November, have tried to claim the case is about the religious freedom of certain corporations, and not contraception. But the case *is* about contraception. The majority in *Hobby Lobby* made this clear, claiming the decision only applies to contraception and not to other things that some religious groups might oppose, such as vaccinations and blood transfusions.

So why are Americans still fighting about something that elsewhere in the industrialized world is a taken-for-granted part of reproductive health care? As Jennifer Reich and I discuss in *Reproduction and Society*, contraception has always had a volatile career in the United States, sometimes being used coercively by those in power, and at other times, like the present, being withheld from those who desperately need it.

The contraceptive wars started with the notorious campaign in the late nineteenth century of Postmaster General Anthony Comstock, who successfully banned the spread of information about contraception under an obscenity statute. Margaret Sanger, who, starting in the early twentieth century, sought to bring birth control information and services to American women, was repeatedly arrested, before her eventual success in starting Planned Parenthood.

Gradually, after the Supreme Court cases mentioned earlier, the discovery and dissemination of the pill and steady increases in premarital sexuality, contraception became far more mainstreamed. Indeed, among its severest critics were feminist health activists of the 1970s, concerned about the safety of early versions of the pill and IUDs, as well as the use of Third World women as "guinea pigs" for testing methods. Federal and state governments became actively involved in the promotion of birth control: Title X of the Public Health Act of 1970 became the first federal program specifically designed to deliver family planning services to the poor and to teens. This legislation in turn drew angry protests from some activists within the African American community who, pointing to the disproportionate location of newly funded clinics in their neighborhoods, raised accusations of "black genocide." (Title X exists to this day, *albeit* chronically underfunded and always threatened with being defunded entirely.)

For a fairly short period after the *Roe v. Wade* decision in 1973, contraception was seen as "common ground" between politicians who were proponents and opponents of that decision. But as the religious right grew more prominent, contraception became increasingly attacked for enabling non-procreative sexual activity.... Moreover, many anti-abortionists have come to reframe some forms of contraception as "abortafacients." Indeed, much of the *Hobby Lobby* case can be understood as a profound disagreement between abortion opponents and the medical community as to what constitutes an actual pregnancy and how particular contraceptives work. . . . The four contraceptive methods at issue in the *Hobby Lobby* case—two brands of emergency contraception and two models of IUDs—are deemed by many conservatives, including the plaintiffs, to cause abortions, while the medical community has gone on record as saying these methods cannot be considered in this light, as they cannot interfere with an established pregnancy. . . .

. . . Though we typically think of contraception as a "women's issue," in fact it plays a huge role in family well-being. A massive literature review by the Guttmacher Institute reveals the negative impacts on adult relationships, including depression and heightened conflict, when births are unplanned, and also shows the health benefits to children when births are spaced.

But the most effective contraceptive methods are the most expensive ones. As Justice Ruth Bader Ginsburg noted in her scathing dissent, the upfront cost of an IUD can be $1,000, nearly a month's wages for a low-income worker. And many women who can't afford an IUD apparently want one. One study has shown that when cost-sharing for contraceptive methods was eliminated for a population of California patients, IUD use increased by 137%. In light of this, my depressing conclusion about the *Hobby Lobby* case is that it follows a familiar pattern of American policies about contraception, and indeed of this country's social policies more generally: the poorest Americans always seem to get the short end of the stick.

This article originally appeared on the Families as They Really Are *blog on July 3, 2014.*

the uneven presence of women and minorities in america's state legislatures—and why it matters

BETH REINGOLD

Women and minorities have made major gains in the ranks of elected U.S. public officeholders—but at all levels of government the progress has been incomplete and uneven. Consider, for example, America's 50 state legislatures. Forty years ago, one would have been hard-pressed to find anyone other than a white man serving in any of these legislatures, yet women and various minorities now claim about one-third of the seats. But there are big variations across the states.

By now, women are about 24% of all state legislators, yet their contingents range from 10% in South Carolina to 40%

in Colorado. African American legislators average 8.1% overall, but the largest contingents (ranging from 20% to 23%) appear in Louisiana, Mississippi, Georgia, and Alabama. Latinos are only 2.9% of all state legislators, and they are concentrated in New Mexico, Texas, California, New York, Nevada, and Arizona.

Apart from population ratios, why do state legislatures vary in diversity—and what difference does it make? Political scientists have made progress in answering these important questions.

opportunities for women

After it became socially acceptable for women to run for office, some observers believed they would make steady progress as male incumbents retired, lost bids for re-election, or moved on to higher posts. But it turns out that states with higher turnover, including states with term limits, have not seen greater gains for women legislators. Other barriers and challenges remain:

- Women make less office-holding progress in states with traditional cultures and strong male-dominated party organizations.
- Female legislators have a stronger presence in states with more liberal electorates and more women in nontra-

ditional social positions. Women are more likely to run for office in such settings and party leaders, voters, and interest groups are more willing to support them.

- Women have a greater presence in "citizen" legislatures that meet infrequently and pay low stipends to their part-time, nonprofessional officeholders. States with multi-member legislative districts also tend to elect more women. Perhaps women find entry easier when the offices are less powerful and there are multiple winners.

overcoming racial and ethnic exclusion

The Voting Rights Act of 1965—and the subsequent use of its provisions to monitor the removal of electoral barriers—has propelled state legislatures toward more closely reflecting the racial and ethnic diversity of state populations. With their rights legally protected, minority electorates can and almost always do elect minority representatives—especially when legislative districts are deliberately designed to encompass majorities of minority voters.

The current situation could be an artificial ceiling for minority legislators, however. To this day, majority-white districts almost always elect white candidates. In the mid-1990s, the Supreme Court began to place limits on the deliberate use of race and ethnicity in drawing district boundaries. Until tools are found to mitigate racial fears and racially polarized voting, dispersing minority voters could cause them to have less leverage in electing minority legislators.

why female and minority legislators matter

Proponents of getting more women and minorities into public office presume that they "make a difference." Scholarly studies have tested various hypotheses and pinpointed key ways in which the presence of female and minority officeholders really does matter.

Most basically, when female and minority citizens see women or co-ethnics in office, they become more politically engaged and empowered. A significant female presence in the legislature increases the chance that women will tell survey researchers they feel they have political influence. Similarly, fellow minorities in office boost African American and Latino voter turnout—and, among Latinos at least, alleviate feelings of political alienation. In all these ways, legislative diversity serves to enhance democratic representation and encourage more inclusive civic engagement.

Inside legislatures, female and minority representatives sponsor distinctive kinds of bills:

- Women are more likely than men to introduce legislation about women's rights and reproductive health choices, and also bills dealing with children, health care, and welfare.

- African American state legislators are more likely (even compared to other Democrats or other representatives with similar constituencies) to introduce measures to combat racial discrimination and boost the socioeconomic and political status of African Africans, as well as measures generally aimed at improving education, health care, and social welfare.
- Latino legislators are most active on issues related to immigration, language learning, and opportunities for migrant laborers.

What about the final votes? The effect of diversity is more ambiguous when it comes to legislative outcomes. One comprehensive study finds that higher percentages of women in state legislatures are associated with the adoption of only eight out of 34 "women-friendly" types of policies. Child support and abortion rights get a boost, according to other studies, but not action to further women's health or protect women from domestic violence.

Yet numerous studies demonstrate that racial and ethnic diversity in state legislatures can result in very significant policy changes on behalf of minority interests. In particular, when powerful leadership positions go to minority legislators—especially to women of color—the prospects improve for legislation to expand access to social welfare programs and increase benefit levels.

This policy brief first appeared on the Scholars Strategy Network *on October 1, 2012.*

part 5: the future of gender

n 1957, two Indiana University professors, writing for the *American Sociological Review*, questioned female college students about their experiences with men on campus. Using the language of the time, they asked if they had ever been "offended" by men's attempts to obtain sexual favors. Over half said they had and 21% said that they at least one man had attempted to force them to have sexual intercourse. More than 50 years later, the statistic has hardly budged—according to the U.S. Department of Justice, one in five college women reports being a victim of a sexual assault—but one thing has changed: We're talking about it. We have college students to thank. It started with Annie Clark and Andrea Pino.

Both students at the University of North Carolina, Clark and Pino were each victimized by fellow students in their first year and faced indifferent or offensive treatment by the college administration. Clark was told that "rape is like a football game" and was encouraged to think of what she might have done wrong. When Pino confessed that she was struggling after her rape, an administrator suggested that perhaps she was just lazy and not cut out for college. Both felt betrayed and helpless.

So they started to consider their options. They discovered that the U.S. Department of Education's Office for Civil Rights had stated that colleges that failed to take reasonable precautions to protect students against sexual assault were violating Title IX, the federal law meant to ensure that women and men have equal access to education. Anyone who felt that the college was in violation could lodge a complaint with the federal government.

Pino and Clark turned to another college student, Dana Bolger, for help. Bolger had been involved in filing a complaint against Amherst. She had been helped by Andrea Brodsky, who filed against Yale. In turn, when Clark and Pino reported the University of North Carolina, they began to help students at other schools.

Eventually it became clear that the problems they encountered at their own schools were common across America. Students experienced high rates of sexual assault alongside flawed policies and incompetent administrators. Colleges were discouraging women from coming forward, burying reports of sexual assault, and giving perpetrators a slap on the wrist. Reporter John Lauerman called college proceedings "antiquated and amateurish... chronically slow, botched and biased." Rapists were graduating, and victims dropping out of school. It was exactly the kind of thing that Title IX was designed to address.

In response, Bolger and Brodsky founded Know Your IX, an organization dedicated to helping students file complaints at their schools. Pino and Clark zigzagged across the country, sleeping in their car and staying up late nights listening to stories, crying with new friends, and helping students all over the country file complaints. By mid-2015, the Office for Civil Rights had received Title IX complaints from over 100 colleges and universities.

Clark and Pino were profiled in *The New York Times*; a film crew started following them around. The White House sat up and took notice, launching a public campaign aimed at helping colleges respond fairly and effectively and pledging, if necessary, to start imposing sanctions until they do. When the documentary *The Hunting Ground* premiered in early 2015, over 1,000 colleges had already requested a screening.

It's easy to think that the fight for gender equality is mostly a thing of the past, but the story of these brave activists reveals otherwise. People are fighting every day to make the world a better place. These efforts are never easy and they are not always successful, but they are how we got here today. They are why women can vote (as of 1920). It's why men can apply for jobs as child care workers and flight attendants (since 1968). It's why we can use birth control (1965)— even if we're not married (1972). It's why women can have credit cards without their husbands' permission (1974) and build a credit history that would allow them to rent an apartment or buy a house on their own. It's why they can enlist in the military (1981) and serve in combat (2013), and marry whomever they want (2015).

Soon, it may be why college campuses are much safer for women and men. There are many other ongoing campaigns, too, aiming to close the pay gap, improve men's ability to balance work and family, make more space for people who don't fit into the gender binary, and much more. The next few articles help us see where we're at and give us some tips on what we can do to make our worlds more equitable.

—LISA WADE

back on track? stall and rebound for gender equality, 1977-2012

**DAVID A. COTTER, JOAN M. HERMSEN,
AND REEVE VANNEMAN**

For almost a decade now, researchers have been struck by a stall in what had been a remarkably rapid and seemingly unstoppable increase in support for gender equity and approval of women's workforce participation up until the mid-1990s. This research paper provides evidence of what may be a rebound in support for gender equity since 2006.

The General Social Survey contains four questions about gender roles that were first posed to the American public in 1977 and have been asked on every survey since 1985. While some of the questions may feel dated (remember they were first asked 37 years ago), they remain useful to show the degree of change in our attitudes about proper roles for men and women. And between 1977 and the mid-1990s, the rate and extent of change were nothing short of remarkable.

- In 1977, 66% of Americans agreed that "It is much better for everyone involved if the man is the achiever outside the home and the woman takes care of the home and family," with just over a third of respondents disagreeing. By 1994, 63% disagreed.
- In 1977, 68% of respondents believed that a preschool child was likely to suffer if her or his mother worked outside the home. By 1994, almost 60% of Americans disagreed.
- In 1977, more than half of respondents (52%) believed that a working mother could not establish as warm a relationship with her children as a full-time homemaker, but by 1994, only 31% of Americans still believed this.
- The percentage of Americans who believed that men and women are equally well suited to politics rose from 48% in 1977 to 75% by 1993.

But in the late 1990s, the trend toward acceptance of new gender roles dipped. The percentage of Americans disagreeing that a woman's place was in the home slipped from 63% in 1994 to 58% in 2000. In the same six years, the number of Americans disagreeing that preschool children were harmed if their mothers worked fell from 57% to 51%, and

Gender Attitudes, 1977–2012

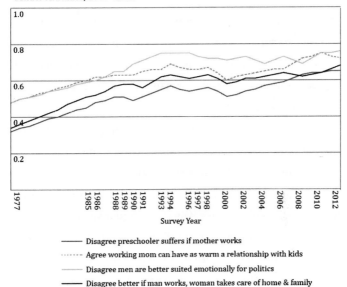

——— Disagree preschooler suffers if mother works

· · · · · · Agree working mom can have as warm a relationship with kids

——— Disagree men are better suited emotionally for politics

——— Disagree better if man works, woman takes care of home & family

Source: Adapted from Cotter et al. 2014
Graphic created for TheSocietyPages.org by Suzy McElrath

Gender Attitudes Scale, 1977–2012

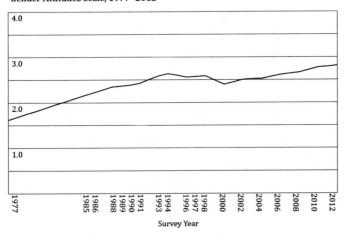

Source: Adapted from Cotter et al. 2014
Graphic created for TheSocietyPages.org by Suzy McElrath

the number agreeing that a working mother could have an equally warm relationship with her child as a full-time homemaker fell from 69% to 60%. Between 1993 and 2004, the percentage of Americans saying that men and women were equally suited to politics fell from 75% to 69%.

... A number of explanations have been put forward for this "stalled revolution," with some attributing it to the economic prosperity of the 1990s and some to the decline of the women's movement, as organized campaigns for better work-family policies gave way to an emphasis on individual solutions, such as "opting out." Other researchers pointed to a rise in cultural conservatism, while still others emphasized the emergence of intensive parenting, based on anxiety about children's chances in an increasingly competitive world.

But our latest analysis shows that since hitting their low points, especially since 2006, there has once more been upward progress in the values associated with approval of new gender roles and relationships. The percentage of people disagreeing that it is better for men to earn the money and women to tend the home rose to an all-time high of 68% in 2012. Less than a third of Americans now say that a male breadwinner family is the ideal arrangement.

In 2000, only about half (51%) of Americans disagreed that preschool children were likely to suffer if their mother worked outside the home, but by 2012, 65% disagreed. The percentage of respondents agreeing that a working mother can establish as warm a relationship with her children had dropped to 60% by 2000 (the same as in 1985), but by 2012 it was back up to 72%. (This was the only attitude question that showed any slippage in the last few years, as it had reached a high of 75% in 2010). And the percentage of respondents saying that men and women are equally suited to politics had rebounded to 76% by 2012.

what lies behind these changes?

The following charts help us explore whether these changes in public attitudes reflect demographic or political changes in the population.

One possibility might be a growing gender gap on these attitudes: that men and women have been changing their views at different rates. But a comparison of trends for each gender does not support this. [See figure on p. 166.] On average, women are slightly more egalitarian than men, but the difference has remained fairly consistent over time. . . .

A second possibility is that these trends are explained by changes in political affiliation or ideology over the period. Perhaps the stall in the mid-1990s represented a swing back toward conservatism in those years, and the restart in

Gender Attitudes by Sex, 1977–2012

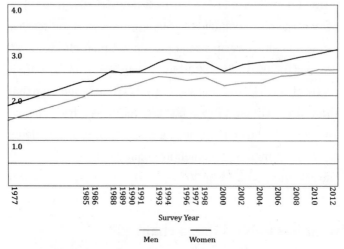

Survey Year

Men   Women

Source: Adapted from Cotter et al. 2014
Graphic created for TheSocietyPages.org by Suzy McElrath

Gender Attitudes by Political Orientation, 1977–2012

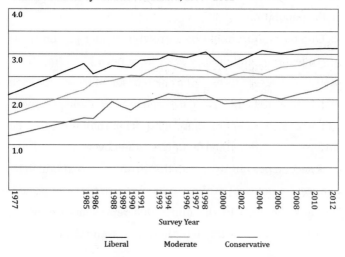

Survey Year

Liberal   Moderate   Conservative

Source: Adapted from Cotter et al. 2014
Graphic created for TheSocietyPages.org by Suzy McElrath

the 2000s a resurgence of liberalism. Although people who describe themselves as "liberal" tend to be more egalitarian and those who are "conservative" are more traditionalist in gender attitudes, the differences between them have not changed much during the entire time period. Furthermore, the same pattern of stalling and restarting can be seen for each group. [See figure on p. 166.]

If anything, the long-term trend has been toward a narrowing rather than a growing gulf between liberals and conservatives on these questions. In fact, during the "restart" of the gender revolution in the 2000s, the greatest increase in the extent of egalitarian views has occurred among conservatives.

The higher people's level of education, the more egalitarian their answers. [See figure on p. 168.] On average, in both 1977 and 2012, people with a bachelor's degree or more scored one point higher than those with less than a high school degree, and one half-point higher than high school graduates. The half-point gap between high school and college graduates in 1977 narrowed for most of the period but since 2000 has opened back up to a half-point difference. The trend over time for education follows the same familiar pattern.

Finally, we look at generational differences in gender attitudes. [See figure on p. 168.] Each subsequent generation has a more egalitarian orientation than the ones before it,

Gender Attitudes by Education, 1977–2012

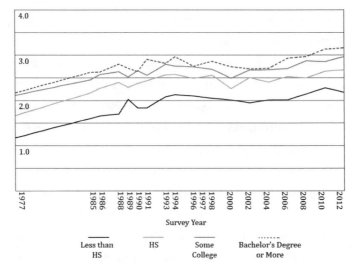

Survey Year

Less than HS | HS | Some College | Bachelor's Degree or More

Source: Adapted from Cotter et al. 2014
Graphic created for TheSocietyPages.org by Suzy McElrath

Gender Attitudes by Cohort, 1977–2012

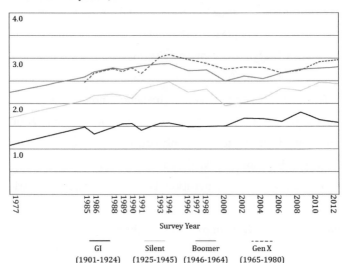

Survey Year

GI (1901-1924) | Silent (1925-1945) | Boomer (1946-1964) | Gen X (1965-1980)

Source: Adapted from Cotter et al. 2014
Graphic created for TheSocietyPages.org by Suzy McElrath

although the gaps progressively decline for the newer generations. The same pattern of upward motion, stall in the 1990s, and then restart is seen in the Silent Generation (born 1925–45), the Baby Boomers (1946–64), and the Gen Xers (1965–1980). But even after the restart, the scores for these generations never exceed their mid-1990s peaks. The restart is real for all these groups, and egalitarian views may continue to rise in all or most, but at this point the main force pulling the overall average up beyond its earlier high point is the entry of the Millennial generation, which displays the most gender-egalitarian attitudes of all.

At this point, it is unclear why the progressive pattern may have resumed. The timing of the major events that might spur period changes—9/11, the Great Recession, etc.—is wrong. But the fact that the restart takes place within generations at approximately the same time suggests that something may have happened—we just don't yet know what.

This paper is part of the Council on Contemporary Families' *Gender Revolution Rebound Symposium. It was published online at the* Council on Contemporary Families *on July 30, 2014.*

three common complaints about political correctness (that completely miss the point)

JARUNE UWUJAREN

My most (and least) favorite thing about the term "political correctness" is that it's basically meaningless.

It's become shorthand for saying "Ideas that I happen to find ridiculous are being taken seriously by a lot of people, and it's ruining this country," which makes its definition entirely subjective, and therefore arbitrary . . .

[Often], political correctness only goes "too far" when it applies to the unfamiliar, the not often talked about, the marginal, the stigmatized.

The thing is, there is nothing so sacred or precious about language or communication that people can't seek ways to be sensitive and inclusive about its use. . . .

Though I understand why people dislike feeling like they must adjust their speech for people they've never thought about, I also wonder if they realize that *we have been doing this to language since time immemorial.* . . . As human knowledge has progressed and political climates have shifted, language has changed to reflect our widening understanding of what is normal, okay, compassionate, and appropriate to say. . . .

For people who are interested in being more sensitive about the use of language as a tool of compassion, these common complaints about "political correctness" look a lot like excuses for ignoring the power and impact of language on social progress.

1. people are too sensitive

What people think they're saying: "People are so self-important nowadays that they think the world has to cater to their sensitivities."

What they're actually saying: "It's okay for the world to cater to the sensitivities of some people, but *this* group of people doesn't count."

The English language normalizes and validates hetero-sexuality, whiteness, maleness, and ability so ubiquitously that people forget that *it reifies these things.* The foundation of the English language was built by white men, and its continued evolution has been largely directed by that same group of people. In other words, what looks like catering to marginalized people is actually decentering a white, male perspective of humankind.

It's true that you don't owe the entire world a certain level of comfort, and you most certainly don't need to manage your life around whether or not a person might be offended by the things you do or say. But if you think that's the point of things like trigger warnings or not making rape jokes, you're mistaken.

Making the decision not to promote language that harms a large group of people—*like victims of violence*—is not particularly hard, compulsory, or overly cautious. It *is*, however, a nice thing to do that costs you nothing. . . .

2. it keeps us from saying what we really mean

What people think they're saying: "People have to constantly walk on eggshells to avoid being labeled bigots. It keeps us from having real conversations and saying what we really mean."

What they're actually saying: "I want the freedom to call people what I please, but no one should call me a bigot."

If you feel that you have to walk on eggshells to avoid being labeled a bigot, you might be in the habit of saying things that are bigoted. I mean, given that even KKK groups deny being racist, it's entirely possible to do and say clearly oppressive things without seeing that they're oppressive. So I'll just say this: If the worst thing you could be called is sexist, racist, homophobic, a bigot, ableist, or the like, you have it pretty good.

Moreover, no one is immune to having prejudices or saying things that expose those prejudices. I may have them, you may have them, and the sooner someone calls us out on them, the sooner we can adjust our attitudes and language to reflect that new understanding.

3. so much focus on words distracts from more important issues

What people think they're saying: "When we pay too much attention to the words people can or can't say, we end up ignoring more important issues."

What they're actually saying: "All issues must be *this* important to ride."

I actually agree that too much focus on nitpicking about what words are acceptable to say can be a distraction. That's why this article isn't a list of feminist-approved words that everyone can agree on.

Being compassionate, forthright, sensitive, honest, and self-aware are all more complicated than knowing the exact right things to say at all times. But that doesn't mean that paying attention to the words we use is something we can afford to ignore: Words are a big deal.

People say that actions speak louder than words, but nothing would ever get done without words because language is literally how we communicate. Speech is a form of action, and the way we speak to and about each other informs the way we treat each other, [which] informs the way we confront injustice. Moreover, the way we talk about people is a reflection of our culture, which can be an issue in itself. Not all forms of violence are physical, and many take the form of words.

There are many words in this world that equate "otherness" with worthlessness. I remember that as a kid, I heard people saying the F-word and D-word (slurs against gays and lesbians) around me all the time. Even after I realized I wasn't straight, these words never made me burst into tears, feel personally offended, or even very angry because they had long since started to seem normal. And *that is a problem.* When kids grow up assuming that slurs used to attack, disparage, and bully them are normal, you have people learning not to fight for themselves when it counts.

Making a conscious decision to avoid these words is about chipping away at the notion that alienating people through language is acceptable in the first place. Victim-blaming language, slurs, and thoughtless words do real harm all the time. They cannot be afterthoughts.

. . . We all encounter new information, people, and ideas that force us to alter our own personal ideas of what's normal. Rather than dismiss the unfamiliar as a burden, we can view it as an opportunity to expand our understanding of who and what matter in this world.

This article originally appeared on Everyday Feminism *on October 27, 2014.*

26

family diversity is the new normal for america's children

PHILIP N. COHEN

People often think of social change in the lives of American children since the 1950s as a movement in one direction—from children being raised in married, male-breadwinner families to a new norm of children being raised by working mothers, many of them unmarried. Instead, we can better understand this transformation as an explosion of diversity, a fanning out from a compact center along many different pathways.

the dramatic rearrangement of children's living situations since the 1950s

At the end of the 1950s, if you chose 100 children under age 15 to represent all children, 65 would have been living in a family with married parents, with the father employed and the mother out of the labor force. Only 18 would have had married parents who were both employed. As for other types of family arrangements, you would find only one child in every 350 living with a never-married mother!

Work-Family Living Arrangements of Children Aged 0–14 in 1960 & 2012

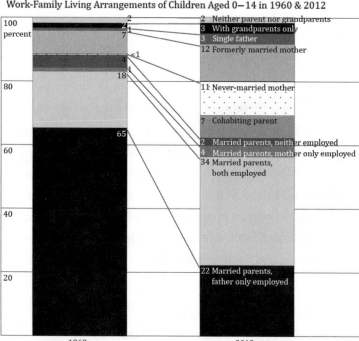

Source: Author calculations from the 1960 US Census and the 2012 American Community Survey, with data from IPUMS.org.
Notes: The Census data only identify one parent per child, so married and cohabiting parent couples are identified by the relationship status of the parent (a married mother, for example, may be married to the biological, adopted, or step father of the child). Single fathers include never-married and formerly-married fathers who are not cohabiting or married. Data includes children aged 0–14. Graphic created for TheSocietyPages.org by Suzy McElrath

Today, among 100 representative children, just 22 live in a married male-breadwinner family, compared to 23 living with a single mother (only half of whom have ever been married). Seven out of every 100 live with a parent who cohabits with an unmarried partner (a category too rare for the Census Bureau to consider counting in 1960), three with a single father, and three with grandparents but no parents. The single largest group of children—34—live with dual-earner married parents, but that largest group is only a third of the total, so that it is really impossible to point to a "typical" family. . . .

To represent this diversity simply, we can calculate the chance that two children picked at random would live in the same work-family structure (among the categories shown on the previous page). In 1960 you would have had an 80% chance that two children, selected at random, would share the same situation. By 2012, that chance had fallen to just a little more than 50-50. The diversity shown here masks an additional layer of differences, which come from the expanding variety of pathways in and out of these arrangements, or transitions from one to another. For example, among the children living with cohabiting parents in 2012, the resident parent is divorced or separated in about a third of cases. In those cases, the cohabiting-parent family often is a blended family with complex relationships to adults and children outside the household. Many more parents have (or raise) children with more than one partner over their lives than in the past, and many more children cycle through several *different* family arrangements as they grow up. The children in America's classrooms today come from so many distinct family arrangements that we can no longer assume they share the same experiences and have the same needs. Likewise, policymakers can no longer design family programs and regulations for a narrow range of family types and assume that they will pretty much meet the needs of all children.

the decline of married couples as the dominant household arrangement

The diversification of family life over time is also shown in the changing proportions of all household types, including ones without children. In the figure [on p. 181], I put each household into one of five types, using census data from 1880 to 2010. The largest category is households composed of married couples living with no one except their own children. If there was any other relative living in a household, I counted it as an extended household. The third category is individuals who live alone. Fourth are single parents (most of them mothers) living with no one besides their own children. In the final category are households made up of people who are not related (including unmarried couples).

As the figure below shows, the married-couple family peaked between 1950 and 1960, when this arrangement characterized two-thirds of households. This was also the peak of the nuclear family, because up until the 1940s, extended families were much more common than they became in the 1950s and 1960s. After that era, the pattern fans out. By 2010, the proportion of married-couple households had dropped to less than half of the total. The proportion of individuals living alone rose from 13% to 27% between 1960 and 2010, and single-parent households rose from 6% to 12%. The result is that households composed of

Distribution of Household Types by Decade, 1880–2010

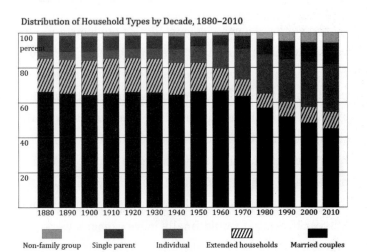

Source: Author calculations with data from IPUMS.org. Data for 1890 is interpolated.
Graphic created for TheSocietyPages.org by Suzy McElrath

lone individuals and single parents accounted for almost 40% of all households by 2010.

Extended households are less common than they were a century ago, mostly as a result of the greater independence of older people, but their numbers have increased again in the last several decades. In sum, the dominant married-couple household of the first half of the twentieth century was replaced not by a new standard but rather by a general increase in family diversity.

how did we get here? market forces, social welfare reform, and family rearrangements

As the market economy generated new products and services that can supplement or substitute for many of the core functional tasks that families had to perform in the past, people became more able to rearrange their family lives. For example, technological innovations made women's traditional household tasks far less time-consuming, while better birth control technology allowed them to control the timing or number of their births. After 1960, employment rates for both married and unmarried women rocketed upward in a 30-year burst that would finally move women's work primarily from the home to the market. The shift to market work reinforced women's independence within their families, but also, in many cases, *from* their families. Women freed from family dependence could live singly, even with children; they could afford to risk divorce; and they could live with a man without the commitment of marriage.

In the aftermath of the Depression and World War II, social reformers increased their efforts to provide a social safety net for the elderly, the poor, and the disabled. The combination of pension and welfare programs that resulted also offered opportunities for more people to structure their lives independently. For older Americans, Social Security benefits were critical. They helped reduce the effective poverty rates of older people from almost 60% in the 1960s to 15% by 2010, freeing millions of Americans from the need to live with their children in old age. . . .

For younger adults, the combination of expanding work opportunities for women and greater welfare support for children made marriage less of a necessity. In the 1960s and 1970s, Aid to Families with Dependent Children grew rapidly, eventually supporting millions of never-married mothers and their children. Welfare did not *create* single mothers—whose numbers rose partly in response to poverty, economic insecurity, and rising incarceration rates, and have continued to rise even after large cutbacks in public assistance—and it *always* carried a shameful stigma while providing a minimal level of monetary support. But it nevertheless allowed poor women to more easily leave abusive or dangerous relationships.

Market forces were most important in increasing the ability of middle-class and more highly educated women to delay, forgo, or leave marriage. Poor women, especially African American women, had long been more likely to work for pay, but their lower earnings did not offer the same personal independence that those with better jobs enjoyed, so welfare support was a bigger factor in the growing ability of poor women to live on their own. Nevertheless, the market has contributed to the growth of single-mother families in a different way over the past 40 years, as falling real wages and increasing job insecurity for less-educated men have made them more risky as potential marriage partners. As a result of these and other social trends, the diversity of family arrangements increased dramatically after the 1950s.

changes in women's work-family situations

The work-family situations of both women and children show the same pattern of increasing diversity replacing the dominant-category system that peaked in the 1950s. The figures [on p. 185] describe women aged 30–34. The rise in education and employment is most dramatic, while marriage and motherhood have become markedly less universal.

Educational, Employment, Marital and Parental Status for Women Aged 30—34 in 1960 & 2012

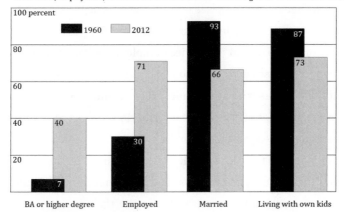

Source: Author calculations from the 1960 US Census and the 2012 American Community Survey, with data from IPUMS.org.
Graphic created for TheSocietyPages.org by Suzy McElrath

Educational, Employment, Marital and Parental Status of Women Aged 30—34 in 1960 & 2012

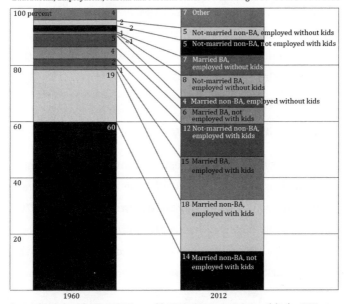

Source: Author calculations from the 1960 US Census and the 2012 American Community Survey, with data from IPUMS.org
Graphic created for TheSocietyPages.org by Suzy McElrath

Rather than simply see each of these as separate trends, we can create profiles by combining the four characteristics into 16 different categories—employed college graduates who are married mothers on one extreme; non-employed non-graduates who aren't married or mothers on the other. In the final figure, I show the distribution across the 10 most common. These clearly show the decline in a single profile— the married, non-college-educated, not-employed mother— and the diversity in statuses that have replaced that single type. In 1960, almost 80% of women in their early thirties had not completed college and were married with children. Now such women comprise less than a third of the total—and no category includes more than 18% of women. In terms of diversity, in 1960 the chance that two women picked at random would be from the same category was 40%. Today that chance has fallen to 11%.

diversity and inequality

Some of the new diversity results from economic changes that are less positive, especially the job loss and wage declines for younger, less-educated men since the late 1970s. In and of itself, however, family diversity doesn't have to lead to inequality. In the Nordic countries of Finland, Norway, and Denmark, for example, unmarried-mother families have poverty rates that barely differ from those of married-couple families—all have poverty rates of less than 10%. Similarly, many countries do a better job of minimizing the school achievement gap between children of single mothers and children of married parents—a study of 11 wealthy countries found the gap is largest in the United States. Different families have different child-rearing challenges and needs, which means we are no longer well served by policies that assume most children will be raised by married-couple families, especially ones where the mother stays home throughout the children's early years. As we debate social and economic policy, we need to consider the needs of children in many different family situations, and how they will be affected by policy changes, rather than privileging one particular family structure or arrangement.

This article was originally published by the Council on Contemporary Families *on September 4, 2014.*

lean in and
1% feminism

LINDA BURNHAM

Feminism almost always needs a modifier.

Since Sheryl Sandberg has taken it upon herself to jump-start the stalled feminist revolution, it's worth taking a look at the brand of feminism she espouses.

Sandberg's book, *Lean In*, together with her plan to relaunch the feminist movement on the scaffolding of *Lean In* Circles, has drawn an enormous amount of media attention. This flows from both Sandberg's prominence as the COO of Facebook and the media's ongoing enchantment with a specific gender story: whether or not women at the top of their professions or careers can "have it all."

To the extent that having it all means having a brilliant, fulfilling, highly compensated career plus a load-bearing partner and a happy home life, that conversation is dead on arrival for the 99%. Most expect to be driven hard, paid little, burdened by debt and, eventually, cast aside. While leaning in at the managers' meeting might move a woman up the corporate jungle gym, it's not going to change the fundamentally exploitative work environments that require workers, male and female, to be chained to their computers and cell phones during every waking hour, devolving to the pathetic state wherein their identities are co-terminus with their job titles. There's no amount of leaning in that will solve the riddle of how to juggle multiple low-wage jobs plus a family. Nearly every working woman who chooses to have children knows that she will spend years of her life scrambling like a maniac, with a partner or without, figuring out infant and child care, after-school care, summer activities for when school is out of session, what to do when the cough turns into a fever, etc.

However endowed we are with confidence, courage, and ambition, short of having the cold hard cash to solve some of these problems by throwing money (and probably some other woman's labor) at them, it's awfully hard to find the wherewithal to lean in.

Nearly all sectors of the feminist movement figured out a long, long time ago that having it all is not an option in the absence of fundamental societal change in the form of institutional policies and structural supports to, at the very least, lighten the unwieldy and disproportionate care-giving load that women still carry. So what is most striking about Sandberg's book is not that a corporate titan found her feminist voice, but that that voice is such a throwback. The battle over the relationship between personal transformation and social change had already been fought, and fought hard, back in the final quarter of the twentieth century. The vast majority of people who claimed any allegiance at all to feminism were clear that, while becoming stronger, more confident women is all to the good, short of substantial society-wide changes (universal access to affordable, high-quality child care, and universal paid parenting leave), having it all is an ever-receding illusion that no amount of leaning in will make real.

Of course, Sandberg is masterful at self-inoculation, and her book is chock full of preemptive moves to immunize against critique. Yes, she graciously grants, not everyone can or wants to have it all. And yes, there are structural barriers that continue to block women's advancement. But, while offering to jump-start and lead a feminist revolution, she has essentially produced a manifesto for corporatist feminism, career advice for the distaff side of the 1%. That advice is, in fact, about how to have it all, while offering precisely zero guidance on how to dismantle the structural barriers to gender equity that still impede most women.

This is not about picking unnecessary fights among the feminist faithful, and there's no need to hate on Sandberg just because she's chosen to expound on what women should do from an especially comfy perch. If the question is how to achieve better gender balance in the upper echelons of corporate management, Sandberg clearly has a contribution to make. Do women sell themselves short and self-sabotage in the corporate world? No doubt. Will Sandberg's book help them devise strategies to advance their careers? Probably so.

But no need to get it twisted. *Lean In* is not about feminism in general, but about a very particular brand of feminism that, delusions aside, has nothing whatsoever to do with inspiring a social movement. We need to understand the core features of the brand, and then decide whether to buy in or take a pass.

Corporatist feminism is fundamentally conservative. It is about conformism to the strictures of corporate culture and requires no qualitative shift in social relations. Instead it requires that those experiencing the impact of inequality and discrimination do some psychological fine-tuning. It is the feminist equivalent of other common story lines about inequality and injustice: Multigenerational poverty? Why, it's the fault of all those poor folk who refuse to disentangle themselves from the "culture of poverty." Ongoing racial discrimination? Actually the problem is all those black folk with chips on their shoulders, mired in the past and ever ready to "play the race card." Gender inequality? If only women would assert themselves, take their seats at the table, commit to putting their careers first, and really lean in. The common theme, whether stated or not: the system is fine, we are the main problem, so let's get down to the real business of tweaking ourselves.

I don't know if Sandberg is a Republican or a Democrat, a Libertarian or a closet Socialist, but this brand of feminism is as conservative as it gets.

1% feminism is all about the glass ceiling, never about the floor. It addresses the concerns, anxieties, and prerogatives of the 1%, women who are at or near the top levels of their professions, the corporate world, or government. Unfortunately, blind to its own limited field of vision, it tends to speak in the name of all women, universalizing that which is profoundly particular.

Trickle-down feminism depends on the benevolence and gender politics of those who make it to the top. It is not about taking collective action or building collective power for change. In Sandberg's example, it took her being pregnant and having to haul her belly across Google's parking lot to realize that the company needed reserved parking for pregnant women. Her position of power facilitated a woman-friendly policy change. Her takeaway from this story: adding more female voices at the highest level expands opportunity and better treatment for all. Maybe, but what if the women at the top have no idea what the women in the middle and at the bottom need or want? Or, even more to the point, what if the interests of women at the top and women at the bottom move in contradictory directions? Women from all levels of society may find common cause on a whole range of gender issues, from parking spaces to wage parity, but certainly we ought to consider whether women in the C-suites are the ones best suited to craft policy for those working the aisles at Home Depot.

Dream-crushing feminism is about stripping feminism of any remnants of a transformative vision. Sandberg says she wants women to dream big, but *Lean In* essentially advocates going along to get ahead. . . . Every progressive social movement worthy of the name is ultimately about a liberatory project that extends outward, beyond those most affected by a particular form of inequity. It calls on each of us to combine with others and to commit our better, more selfless, justice-loving selves to building a society that lifts up the full humanity of all who have suffered discrimination, indignities, oppression, exploitation, abuse. When we're haggling over the politics of the kitchen, the bedroom, the boardroom, or the congressional hearing room, that liberatory project can seem exceedingly remote and far-fetched. But, while we need to be pragmatic and tough enough to gain ground on feminist issues in an inhospitable political climate, we also need to keep a broader transformative vision alive. Reducing that vision to tips on career advancement is not a way to jump-start a movement—it cuts away at its heart.

Being clear about Sandberg's brand surely wouldn't matter much if the feminist movement were in better shape, represented by more varied voices and stronger organizations. Sandberg's voice would be just one among many advocating different roads toward more equitable gender relations. But the fact that Sandberg has occupied so much space and is taken so seriously as the new voice of feminism is a sign of how intractably conservative the current political environment is. That's all the more reason to reassert the social justice roots of feminism, and to make sure that it does not become synonymous with leaning in.

This article originally appeared on Portside *on March 26, 2013.*

shattering the glass ceiling for women in politics

PAMELA O'LEARY AND SHAUNA SHAMES

The United States is a country of astonishing diversity, yet public offices continue to be overwhelmingly dominated by white men. Women are 51% of the population but make up only 24% of state legislatures, 18% of Congress and big-city mayors, and 10% of state governors. Progress toward increasing women's share of public offices has been slow and at times reversed. Women's underrepresentation raises questions of justice and, according to available research, undermines the optimal functioning of democratic government. Female officeholders raise different issues, forge compromises more readily, and give voice to the needs of families and vulnerable groups in our society. Girls and women also yearn to see people like them in office, and underrepresentation of any group can make government and its actions seem less legitimate or "out of touch." This brief draws on available research to suggest ways to boost women's presence at all levels of government.

slow progress and gender gaps in political ambition

State legislative seats are a crucial place to look to chart women's progress, because campaigns for national offices are often launched by such legislators. Since the mid-1990s, women have increased their share of state legislative seats by only three percentage points, going from 21% of state legislative seats in 1994 to 24% now. In 2010, moreover, women lost ground in state legislatures for the first time in decades. Term limits, once believed to give women more opportunity, ended up forcing previously elected women out of office. And additional women legislators were not elected in equal or greater numbers—in significant part because not so many women ran for office that year. The picture was brighter in 2012, with a record number of women elected to political office nationwide. Even so, at the current growth rate, gender parity in Congress will not be achieved for 500 years.

Some scholars point to a gender gap in political ambition as the most significant barrier to increasing the number of women in office. When equally qualified women and men are surveyed, women are much more unlikely to report wanting to run for office—even though when women do run, they win elections at the same rates as male candidates. Overall, the main problem is that not enough women are running. Based on what is known, there are three promising strategies to help turn that around.

1. ask females to run early and often

The earlier a candidate begins to run for office, the better his or her chances of climbing the political ladder. Twelve of the last 19 U.S. presidents started their political careers before age 35. When the path to achieve significant political influence and chair a committee is based on seniority, a candidate benefits from being elected when young. Additionally, over 40% of the women who currently serve in Congress served in student government in their youth. However, one of us (Shauna Shames) finds that even those women who dominated student government in high school turn away from politics in college; men also show more political ambition during graduate school. Girls and young women need to learn at a young age that politics is a good place for them to change the world. As Elizabeth Warren repeatedly told girls during her campaign, "I'm running for Senate, because that's what girls do!"

As girls become women, they have to be encouraged repeatedly to run for office. On average, researchers have found, women need to be asked to run seven times before they seriously consider launching candidacies. Fortunately, many nonprofits are getting involved in helping girls and young women learn to lead and training them to run effective election campaigns.

2. a presidential commission on gender and inclusive democracy

In no country have women reached equality without help from the government. In our country, President John F. Kennedy's Commission on the Status of Women in the 1960s helped spur the modern feminist movement and identified governmental actions that could alleviate discrimination against women. We suggest the same approach now, concentrating on women in elective and appointed politics.

A new presidential commission could take seriously the global rallying cry that democracy without women is not democracy. In our international dealings, we push governments to ensure participation by women, yet the United States ranks 81st in percentage of women serving in the national legislature. The racially and politically diverse membership of a new commission should include elected leaders and representatives of an array of organized groups seeking to increase the number of women in office. Drawing on growing bodies of research, the commission could document trends, opportunities, and obstacles and recommend new ways to encourage participation and office holding by women, people of color, and others currently underrepresented at the city, county, state, and federal levels.

3. stronger action by political parties

Both major U.S. political parties already ensure that 50% of convention delegates are women, and both parties would gain by taking further steps to recruit and support women as candidates. Of course, it is far easier for the Democratic and Republican National Committees to mandate gender balance for delegates than for candidates and nominees in elections. But parties could still encourage and recruit women far more actively than they currently do.

National party officials could create target deadlines; for example, committing to have at least 30% of their candidates for national offices be women by 2020. Similarly, the national political parties could create funds to be dispersed to state and local parties that do a better job of recruiting and nominating diverse candidates. In Norway, for example, no more than 60% of corporate board members can come from one gender. U.S. political parties could use financial rewards to prod state and local parties toward similar patterns of candidate balance.

If more women are urged to run for office, we know that more will win and serve, making American democracy more representative and more effective. It is time for stronger efforts to break the gender glass ceiling in politics.

This article was originally published by the Scholars Strategy Network *in November 2013.*

children's gender self-determination: a practical guide

JANE WARD

S o you want to have a kid, or you want to interact with kids, but you're not a big fan of the gender binary and the 10 trillion ways children are asked to conform to it, nor do you like the way that gender identity is offered to children as the primary way to make sense of themselves, and you're also irked by the fact that even the children's books that emphasize gender nonconformity (like *My Princess Boy*) fail to distinguish between "girls' clothes" and "clothes marketed to girls"? Okay, me too. Read on!

In my online magazine, *Feminist Pigs*, I've tried to argue for the importance of providing *all children*—not just those who "show the signs" of gender nonconformity—with the social, cultural, and political tools they can use to simultaneously work with and against the gender binary. Providing children with gender self-determination involves two efforts: (1) parents' active cultivation of children's familiarity with and appreciation for genderqueer imagery, language, bodies, politics, and subculture; and (2) welcoming children's engagement with gender signifiers (gendered colors, toys, objects, images, feelings, and modes of relating) without "gender diagnosis," or the imposition of meaning about what children themselves are signifying—about their identities or their nature.

To my mind, gender self-determination introduces children to the relational and culturally embedded pleasures associated with gender play without concretizing a gendered selfhood. It recognizes that neither children nor the world are "gender neutral." Nor are any of our genders "independent" from the cultures in which we are located; hence I think the term "gender independent," which is gaining some momentum in Toronto, is a great first step but cannot quite capture the project I'm interested in. Working for gender self-determination is about operating with the presumption that no single child has a greater innate capacity for gender creativity or fluidity or independence than another. All children have this potential. . . .

It's challenging to implement these ideas because the world presents us with obstacles at every step, because we have very few models for how to relate to children in genderqueer ways, and because the stakes and risks are extremely high (someone may very well call child protective services and report that you are enacting a queer "social experiment" on your child). So here are some guidelines I have developed in conversation with some brave and amazing parents, students, and friends.

1. **don't refer to kids as boys and girls.** Thankfully, many parents are starting to resist gender stereotyping and allow for cross-gender exploration, often in the form of providing children with "dress up" clothes that allow for a broader range of play (male children in princess gowns, girls in Spider-Man attire, etc.). But the vast majority of parents unthinkingly refer to their children as girls and boys without considering the ways this makes sex/gender the central component of how kids think of themselves, understand their social group, and view themselves through their parents' eyes. I can think of only two reasons to refer to children as if you know their gender identity: (1) You are doing some feminist/queer strategizing about how to combat the ways that children are diminished according to their *perceived* genders. (2) You need to talk about children's bodies for medical or other practical reasons, which isn't actually

about gender anyway. If you need to talk about vaginas or penises, just do that.

I have only once referred to my two-year-old kid, Yarrow, as "a boy," and it was when a child at a park asked me, "Is that a boy or a girl?" and I panicked. Later, I talked with the brilliant Kathy Witterick about how to handle this, and she suggested answering the question with, "That's Yarrow." Ah! So simple. You can also say, "That's a question you should ask Yarrow." . . . It's a good way to go with older kids, because it allows them to answer for themselves and avoids treating the answer like it's self-evident. . . . The challenge is balancing your obligation to provide your child with gender self-determination with the importance of lovingly interacting with other kids for whom genderqueerness may be a new idea.

Similarly, when talking about more than one child, don't call children "the boys" or "the girls." Don't use terms like "buddy" or "dude" or "precious" unless you use these words to describe all children, regardless of your perception of their gender, or unless you mix it up in a cool way (e.g., "princess dude") or you alternate (e.g., call your kid "dude" on Tuesday, "princess" on Wednesday).

2. **queer your kid.** Buy clothing or acquire hand-me-down clothing marketed to both boys and girls. If you have a

child with a penis, do not refer to clothes marketed to girls, such as dresses, as "special" or "costumes" or "dress up"; this reinforces their strangeness or difference.... Until your kid is old enough to create their own gendered style, aim for androgyny or alternate butch and femme aesthetics on different days. If your child has a vagina, the world expects long hair, so perhaps give this kid the experience of short hair before the weight of the gender binary comes crashing down in preschool. This, combined with pants, will mean that everyone will relate to your kid as a boy. You can go with that, you can mix it up, you can avoid the temptation to rescue your kid from what you might imagine is "misrecognition," but you really have no idea what your kid's gender is until they tell you, so I say just calm down, breathe deep, and observe. What you *do* know is that all children will encounter the gender binary soon enough, so what you can offer in the meantime is an early familiarity with gender fluidity.

3. **don't diagnose your kid.** Don't announce that despite your best feminist/queer efforts, your child is simply "a girly girl" or a "boy's boy." Do not make up a narrative about your child's gender, and do not believe that your child's own gendered narratives are fixed or have the

same meaning to your child that they have to you. Let's say you have a child with a vagina who is obsessed with princesses. Avoid the temptation to say things like, "We've really tried to steer her away from princess stuff, but she's just a girly girl no matter what we do." If you have a child with a penis who turns paper towels into weapons at every turn, don't say, "Gosh, I hate to admit it, but I guess testosterone really *does* have all the effects they say it does!" This may shut down or misrecognize whatever queer or feminist meanings that could be present within princess play or paper towel aggression, and it also fails to recognize that your child's gender will evolve over time and may be stifled by any worrying and labeling on the part of nearby adults. Redirect kids away from violence and toward human connection, but don't make any of it about gender.

4. **change the words in kids' books.** Rarely do I read a book to Yarrow without changing any of the words. While reading, I frequently change "he" to "she," as the former is terribly overused in kids' books as a universal pronoun to describe all animals and most people. I also will use "he" on one page and "she" on the next page to describe the same character, because, well, some people identify as both male and female. I change man/woman and boy/

girl to "person," "kid," "the narrator," "our protagonist," "the soccer player," etc. I change "girls' toys" to "toys marketed to girls." To introduce genderqueerness where there never is any, I sometimes refer to the people who appear to be mothers in a given story as "daddies" (I learned this from Yarrow, who really likes to mix it up!). I know it seems stuffy, but I like the way it teaches kids that we default to gender when we really mean something far more specific or complex. . . .

5. **when an important adult thinks they need to know your kid's gender, ask why.** It's less popular these days for schools to gender segregate children or speak openly about children's gender differences than it once was, but it *is* common for schools to proudly talk about the importance of "gender balance" as a form of diversity. But we need to ask why this is important. To me it reveals that the school expects kids to have a clearly defined gender and that they think gender is revealing something important about who kids are. We need to push back on that idea. When I went to Toys "R" Us and asked a salesperson where I could find a plastic pool and was met with the response, "For a boy or a girl?", that was obviously ludicrous. But far more insidious are all of the medical records and preschool applications we have encountered

that require us to label Yarrow as either a boy or a girl. We've started asking, "Do we really need to answer this question? And if so, why?" We're often bullied into answering it, but at the very least we have raised the question.

This article originally appeared on Feminist Pigs *on February 16, 2012.*

discussion guide and group activities

1. A sociological understanding of gender is that gender is "socially constructed" and takes "work" to reproduce. Find three to four examples in this volume of how people have "worked" at constructing or deconstructing their gender. What did they do? Why did they do it? How do you think it might have affected how others see them? Think of some examples from your own life where you or those around you "do gender" on a daily basis. What are your motivations and strategies? Consider both the pleasure of doing gender and its coercive power.

2. Had you thought about the skirt lengths in "The Balancing Act of Being Female" (Chapter 8) before? Have you or someone you've observed ever miscalculated and felt inappropriate or out of place? How do the norms around skirt lengths relate to the use of high heels as a form of distinction in "High Heels and Distinction among Women" (Chapter 11)? What about norms for how much

cleavage is visible? When doing the balancing act, women have to balance all three together. How so? What are some other types of clothing and physical markers that denote membership in a category? Do we also "do" race, class, sexual orientation, American-ness, and other identities? How does doing those things interact with how we do gender, making the balancing act all the more complicated?

3. As a complement to the pieces on men's and women's breasts in the "Ideas" section—"Why Breastfeeding in Public Is Taboo" (Chapter 3) and "Tits (The Story of My Man-Boobs)" (Chapter 2)—read "What Makes a Body Obscene?" (http://thesocietypages.org/socimages/2011/12/27/what-makes-a-body-obscene/). Together, what do these stories tell us about how we perceive male and female bodies? In some cultures, women's breasts are not as sexualized as they are in the United States. What are some of the consequences of this? What other body parts carry gendered meanings? And how do we manage those body parts to try to fit into the gender binary? Or, alternatively, like the author of "Tits," how do we learn to flaunt in order to disrupt it?

4. Discuss how enabling a child's "gender self-determination" (Chapter 29) might erode our tendency to adopt "gender constancy" (Chapter 1). How might efforts toward "queer parenting" be constrained by gendered institutions and deeply ingrained cultural assump-

tions about the gender binary? Which way of learning about gender—self-determination or constancy—most reflects what you learned as a child? How you feel now? Would you try "genderqueer parenting" with your own children (now or in the future)? Why or why not?

5. Read the Scholars Strategy Network brief (http://thesocietypages.org/ssn/2014/09/15/how-gender-inequality-persists/) about why gender inequality persists in the modern world. Do you think we are more or less gender egalitarian today than we were 20 years ago? Craft an answer using three empirical studies from this volume to support your argument. Feel free to explore an answer that includes both a yes and a no. For people who will be advocating for gender equality in the near future, what do you think are the most pressing issues? Why? What kind of research could be done to support their efforts? What cultural and institutional changes do you think would be most helpful?

6. Listen to the Office Hours podcast "Leta Hong Fincher on Gender Inequality in China." Compare and contrast the history of gender equality in China with the history of gender equality in the United States detailed in the piece "Back on Track? Stall and Rebound for Gender Equality, 1977–2012" (Chapter 24).

7. How do the problems of gender equity in politics described in "Shattering the Glass Ceiling for Women in

Politics" (Chapter 28) relate to the problems of women in business in "*Lean In* and 1% Feminism" (Chapter 27)? What is similar about the corporate and the political worlds, and what is different? What are your career aspirations? What is your orientation toward a political career? Do you think either of these are affected by your gender? Why or why not? Do you think reading this book might change what you think is possible for yourself? How so?

8. Read "Gender and Biased Perceptions: Scientists Rate Job Applicants" (Chapter 16). If you were a hiring manager, what could you do to try and eliminate this type of bias? What changes would be needed to eliminate these inequalities at the level of an organization or a country?

9. Read "Coming to Terms with Being a Working-Class Academic" (http://thesocietypages.org/sociologylens/2015/04/22/coming-to-terms-with-being-working-a-working-class-academic/) and think about how it relates to the "Is the 'Mrs.' Degree Dead?" (Chapter 20) piece in this volume. How might George Byrne's perspective on class differences relate to how college is experienced by people from different backgrounds? Do you think some kinds of women might be more likely to think of college as a route to a ring? Which ones and why? Have you ever thought of your time in college as a romantic opportu-

nity? Or your degree as an attractive quality in the dating game? Did you or your family members consider your potential marriage prospects when you picked a college? Why or why not?

10. Gender quotas that require a certain percentage of women in elected office or on corporate boards, for example, are the law in some countries. Thinking about the piece "The Uneven Presence of Women and Minorities in America's State Legislatures—And Why It Matters" (Chapter 23), discuss the pros and cons of using quotas in the United States.

11. Listen to the Office Hours Podcast "Victor Rios on Policing Black and Latino Boys." How does the intersectionality of race, class, and gender, introduced in the opening of Part 3, "Inequalities," work to produce the inequalities described by Rios? How can you use Gerke's concept of marginalized masculinities in "Gay Male Athletes and Discourses of Masculinity" (Chapter 4) to understand the experiences of these youths?

activities

GENDER AS A COMMODITY

Gender stereotypes are widely used in advertisements. Even when gender stereotypes are challenged and joked about in the media, the goal is usually to sell products to a wider range of people. After scrolling through Lisa Wade's long list of "Pointlessly Gendered Products" on The Society Pages or the *Sociological Images* Pinterest page (https://www.pinterest.com/socimages/pointlessly-gendered -products/), have the group members find a current advertisement in which gender stereotypes are either reinforced or subverted to sell a product. Have each person present their advertisement and discuss the following questions as a group:

1. How are gender stereotypes used to sell products in these examples? Do you find them effective?
2. How do attempts to challenge gender stereotypes get co-opted by advertising companies to sell products? Do you notice gender more in these types of ads than in ads that call on more traditional gender roles?
3. Does the commodifying of new gender identities hinder or further gender equality? How so?

What's wrong with gendered products? Read "Five Reasons Why Pointlessly Gendered Products Are a Problem" (http:// thesocietypages.org/socimages/2015/01/20/five-reasons-why-pointlessly-gendered-products-are-a-problem/) and discuss.

OTHER ACTIVITIES FROM THE SOCIETY PAGES

The Society Pages offers a range of teaching exercises and classroom and group discussion activities on its Teaching TSP blog. Here are a few that might be fun and provocative for your group:

1. "Summer Lovin' and the Sexual Double Standard," by Erin Hoekstra. This piece tackles some of the issues of hooking up on campus (including whether hookups are, as many believe, bad for women).
2. "The Rhetoric and Reality of Opting Out," by Kia Heise. A discussion starter on women's paths into and out of the market labor force, including how those paths differ from those taken by earlier generations.
3. "The Mating Game," by Hollie Nyseth Brehm. This activity helps illustrate the issue of mate selection and family formation while asking participants to consider gender, sexuality, and the life course.

about the contributors

Tristan Bridges is in the sociology department at The College at Brockport, State University of New York. He studies men and masculinities, particularly with respect to changes in U.S. gender relations.

Linda Burnham is an author and activist who publishes on African-American women, African-American politics, and feminist theory. In 2005, she was nominated as one of 1,000 Peace Women for the Nobel Prize.

Philip N. Cohen is a sociologist at the University of Maryland–College Park and co-editor of *Contexts*. He is the author of *The Family: Diversity, Inequality, and Social Change* (W. W. Norton, 2014) and blogs at *Family Inequality*.

Nicki Lisa Cole is a public sociologist and the founder of *21st Century Nomad*, a digital sociology magazine. Her current research focuses on the brand power, consumer culture, and supply chain of Apple, Inc.

D'Lane Compton is in the sociology department at The University of New Orleans. She studies social psychology, demography and sexual orientation, and methodology and research design.

Cheryl Cooky is in the department of American studies and the department of women's, gender, and sexuality studies at Purdue University. She studies the sociology of sport, female athletes, and gendered media representations.

Matt Cornell is an artist, performer, and film programmer who lives and works in Los Angeles.

David A. Cotter is in the sociology department at Union College. He studies stratification and inequality.

Tressie McMillan Cottom is in the sociology department at Virginia Commonwealth University. She is the author of *Lower Ed: How For-Profit Colleges Deepen Inequality in America* (The New Press, 2016).

Shari L. Dworkin is in the department of social and behavioral sciences at the University of California, San Francisco. She studies HIV/AIDS prevention and gender relations.

Tara Fannon is in the political science and sociology program at the University of Ireland, Galway. She studies masculinity, disability, identity, and the body.

Markus Gerke is in the sociology program at Stony Brook University (State University of New York). He studies race, class, and gender, as well as the intersections of whiteness and masculinity in politics and sports.

Kjerstin Gruys is a Thinking Matters fellow and a postdoctoral scholar at the Clayman Institute for Gender Research at Stanford University. She studies the relationship between physical appearance and social inequality.

Laura T. Hamilton is in the sociology department at the University of California, Merced. She is the author, with Elizabeth A. Armstrong, of *Paying for the Party: How College Maintains Inequality* (Harvard University Press, 2013).

Douglas Hartmann is in the sociology department at the University of Minnesota. His research interests focus on race and ethnicity, multiculturalism, popular culture (including sports and religion), and contemporary American society. He is coeditor of The Society Pages.

Erin Hatton is in the department of sociology at the State University of New York at Buffalo. She is the author of *The Temp Economy: From Kelly Girls to Permatemps in Postwar America* (Temple University Press, 2011).

Joan M. Hermsen teaches sociology and gender studies at the University of Missouri. She studies inequality, labor markets, gender, and quantitative methods.

Carole Joffe is a professor at the Bixby Center for Global Reproductive Health at the University of California, San Francisco, and is a professor emerita of sociology at the University of California, Davis. She is the author of *Dispatches from the Abortion Wars: The Costs of Fanaticism to Doctors, Patients, and the Rest of Us* (Beacon Press, 2011).

Christin Munsch is in the department of sociology at the University of Connecticut. She studies family, work and occupations, gender, social psychology, and quantitative methods.

Pamela O'Leary is in the human and organizational development program at Fielding Graduate University. She is also an organizational and international government consultant in women's leadership development, with a focus on millennials and youth.

C.J. Pascoe is in the sociology department at the University of Oregon. She is the author of *Dude, You're a Fag: Masculinity and Sexuality in High School* (University of California Press, 2011).

Beth Reingold is in the department of political science at Emory University. She is the author of *Representing Women: Sex, Gender, and Legislative Behavior in Arizona and California* (University of North Carolina Press, 2000).

Virginia Rutter is in the department of sociology at Framingham State University. She studies families, sexuality, and diversity, including relationships, inequality, and family policy.

Mimi Schippers is in the department of sociology at Tulane University. She is the author of *Polyqueer: Compulsory Monogamy and the Queer Potential of Plural Sexualities* (New York University Press, 2015).

Shauna Shames is in the department of political science at Rutgers-Camden. She studies race, gender, and politics.

Gwen Sharp is Associate Dean of Liberal Arts and Sciences at Nevada State College. She studies technology and innovation in agriculture and racial and ethnic minorities' rural landownership.

Christopher Uggen is in the sociology department at the University of Minnesota. He studies crime, law, and deviance, especially how former prisoners manage to put their lives back together. He is coeditor of The Society Pages.

Jarune Uwujaren is an independent author and editor who studied at Georgia State University.

Reeve Vanneman is in the sociology department at the University of Maryland. He studies gender inequality.

Lisa Wade is in the sociology department at Occidental College. She is the author, with Myra Marx Ferree, of *Gender: Ideas, Interactions, Institutions* (W. W. Norton, 2014).

Tina Pittman Wagers is a clinical psychologist who teaches psychology at the University of Colorado, Boulder.

Jane Ward is in the department of gender and sexuality studies at the University of California, Riverside. She is the author of *Not Gay: Sex between Straight White Men* (New York University Press, 2015).

Index

Note: Italicized page locators indicate figures.